PINNACLE STUDIO

NICK VANDOME

In easy steps is an imprint of Computer Step
Southfield Road . Southam
Warwickshire CV47 0FB . United Kingdom
www.ineasysteps.com

Notice of Liability
Every effort has been made to ensure that this book contains accurate and current information. However, Computer Step and the author shall not be liable for any loss or damage suffered by readers as a result of any information contained herein.

Trademarks
Microsoft and Windows are registered trademarks of Microsoft Corporation. Pinnacle Systems, the Pinnacle Systems logo and Studio are trademarks/registered trademarks of Pinnacle Systems, Inc. All other trademarks are acknowledged as belonging to their respective companies.

Printed and bound in the United Kingdom

ISBN 1-84078-267-6

Contents

Introducing Pinnacle Studio

Pinnacle Studio is one of the leading consumer level digital video editing programs on the market. It gives a mass market audience the chance to enjoy the excitement and versatility of digital video, one of the fastest growing areas in the digital world. This chapter gives an overview of digital video and also shows how to get started with Pinnacle Studio.

Covers

Chapter One

Digital video overview

General

Until recently, digital video capture and editing was very much the domain of professional film-makers and editors. However, due to a considerable drop in price of the hardware and dramatically improved performance and ease of use of the software, digital video is now very much a mass market product. Working with digital video consists of three main elements:

- Capture. This can be done with a digital video (DV) camera and then downloaded directly onto a computer. In addition, analog video can also be used, in which case an analog to digital convertor unit is used to convert the video into a digital format, which can then be edited on a computer

- Editing. This is when the digital footage is edited on a computer. Unwanted footage can be deleted and elements such as titles, transitions, sound effects, narration and music can be added. This is where a digital video editing program like Pinnacle Studio comes into its own. It offers considerable power and versatility and this is one of the most creative and enjoyable parts of working with digital video

- Publishing. Once footage has been edited it can then be published in a variety of output formats. It can be saved in a standard digital video format for playback on a computer, it can be saved onto a CD or DVD, or it can be saved for publication on the Web. Pinnacle Studio has the facility to produce all of these output formats

The TV standards settings can be selected during the point of capture in Pinnacle Studio. To do this, click on the Settings button on the Diskometer in the Capture window and select the Capture Source tab. Then select the required standard in the TV Standard box.

TV standards

Most digital video will be used at some stage for display on a television. This could be directly from the camera, or via a DVD or CD. Depending on where you are in the world, televisions use different standards for broadcasting. The two main ones are:

- NTSC. This stands for National Television Standards Committee. It is used primarily in North America and also some parts of Asia

- PAL. This stands for Phase Alternation Line and is used primarily in Western Europe, Australasia and Japan

A higher resolution for each frame of video footage also creates a larger file size.

Resolution

This relates to the physical size of a frame of video. The higher the resolution, the larger the image. However, this also leads to an increase in file size. For some video formats the resolution can be set in the editing software during downloading or publishing. The resolution of video footage is initially set by the resolution of the digital camera being used to capture the footage.

Compression

Raw digital video takes up an enormous amount of hard disc space when it is downloaded from a video camera. In order to make this more manageable for the published output, varying degrees of compression can be applied to reduce the file size. This inevitably has an adverse affect on the quality of the video and it is a question of balancing this against the reduced file size. Different video file formats use different methods of compression and three of the most common are:

If you are going to be publishing video on the Web, or sending it by email, make sure it is as compressed as much as possible, otherwise it will take too long to download. This usually involves creating the final file using the Windows Media Player or Real Media codec for compression.

- MPEG-1. This compresses video at a resolution rate of 352x240 and is commonly used for producing VCDs

- MPEG-2. This compresses video at a variety of resolution rates, but generally 480x480. It is commonly used for producing S-VCDs and DVDs

- DV. This compresses video at a resolution rate of 720x480 and is commonly used for copying video back onto a tape in a digital video camera

Codecs

Codecs (which is a contraction of COmpressor and DECompressor) are items of software that are used to compress video for storage and then decompress them for playing. There are a variety of codecs currently in use, including:

MPEG stands for Motion Pictures Experts Group.

- MPEG-1

- MPEG-2

- Real Media

- Windows Media Video

Digital video hardware

Digital video is a medium that requires a certain amount of hardware before you can start thinking about an editing program such as Pinnacle Studio.

Digital video cameras

Digital video cameras have dramatically fallen in price in recent years so that they are now realistically affordable for most users. In general, they operate in a similar way to analog video cameras and some areas to look at include:

Some digital video cameras come bundled with the full version of Pinnacle Studio.

- Pixel count. Digital video cameras capture images on a CCD (Charge Coupled Device). Look for a camera that has a CCD that can capture in the range of 800,000 pixels (short for picture elements) per frame upwards

- Processor enhancements. Once an image has been captured on the camera's CCD, it is conveyed to the tape via the systems processor. Some models are marketed with enhancements to these processors to improve the quality

- Memory card. Most digital video cameras can also capture still images through the use of a memory card in the format of SmartMedia or CompactFlash

Analog video camera

If you already own an analog video camera the footage can be converted into digital and then edited on a computer with Pinnacle Studio. However, if you are looking to buy a new video camera, it would be best to go for a digital one.

Pinnacle Studio is only available for use on a PC but not an Apple Mac.

Computer

When working with digital video on a PC look for the following minimum requirements:

- 1 GHz processor

- 256 MB of memory

- 80 GB hard drive

If possible, use a computer with the maximum amount of memory and hard drive space available.

...cont'd

FireWire card

The standard method of downloading digital video onto a computer is through a FireWire card. This is a technology that was first developed by Apple Computers and it offers a much faster rate of data transfer than the USB method. FireWire is also known under its international standard name of IEEE 1394, while Sony use the title i-Link to describe the same thing. FireWire cards can be bought individually and inserted into a spare PCI slot in a Windows based PC.

There are different options when buying Pinnacle Studio and some of these include a FireWire card in the package.

FireWire cards can be used to download digital video from a digital video camera into a computer

Analog to digital conversion unit

Three analog to digital conversion units to look at are: Dazzle Hollywood Bridge from Dazzle at www.dazzle.com; Directors Cut from Miglia at www.miglia.com; and Canopus AVDC–100 from Canopus at www.canopus.com

Also known as digitizers, analog to digital conversion units are used to convert analog video into a digital format that can then be downloaded and edited on a computer. These units are connected to the analog video camera and also the computer and generally the converted video is downloaded onto the computer via a FireWire connection. There are a variety of these units on the market and some Pinnacle products have them bundled with the Studio program.

CD Writer

VCD stands for VideoCD and S-VCD stands for Super-VideoCD.

CD writers enable you to copy, or burn, completed movies onto CDs. These come as either internal or external units and can be used to create VCDs and S-VCDs i.e. digital video formats created on CDs.

DVD Writer

DVD writers enable you to burn completed movies onto DVDs. Like CD writers, they also come as either internal or external units. Although they are considerably more expensive than CD writers, their price has been falling consistently and they are now a realistic option for most people.

About Pinnacle Studio

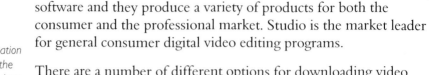

Pinnacle is one of the leading manufacturers of digital video editing software and they produce a variety of products for both the consumer and the professional market. Studio is the market leader for general consumer digital video editing programs.

More information about all of the Pinnacle products can be found on their website at www.pinnaclesys.com

There are a number of different options for downloading video and publishing it in a digital format. These include downloading analog video, downloading digital video, downloading onto a desktop PC and downloading onto a laptop. To cater for all of these combinations, Studio comes bundled in a variety of ways. These include:

- Studio. The full version of the software that can be used to capture, edit and publish analog and digital video

For use with a laptop a PCMCIA card is used for the FireWire connection, rather than a PCI one used on a PC.

- Studio DV. Full version of Studio and a FireWire card

- Studio AV/DV. Similar to Studio DV except that it can input analog video

- Studio AV/DV Deluxe. Full version of Studio plus a FireWire card and an analog to digital conversion unit

- Studio MovieBox USB. Full version of Studio plus a USB conversion unit for downloading analog video

- Studio MovieBox DV. Full version of Studio plus external devices for downloading digital and analog video

Input formats

Pinnacle Studio can also capture analog video. For this an analog to digital conversion unit is required or an analog to digital capture card. The Studio AV/DV, AV/DV Deluxe and MovieBox DV packages include hardware for downloading analog video.

The most common formats for obtaining video in Pinnacle Studio are:

- DV. Also known as MiniDV, this is the most common format for capturing digital video with a digital video camera

- Digital8. This is a digital version of the analog Hi8 format

- MicroMV. This is a relatively new digital video format and it is used mainly by Sony in its range of digital video cameras. Studio is one of the few video editing programs that supports the MicroMV format

Output formats

Once video has been edited with Pinnacle Studio, the completed movie can be published in a variety of formats:

In order to copy digital video back to the video camera in DV or Digital8 format, the camera has to have a DV Input function.

- DV or Digital8 tape

- VideoCD (VCD)

- Super VideoCD (S-VCD)

- DVD

- MPEG-1 and MPEG-2

- AVI

- RealVideo

The VCD and S-VCD formats can be used to burn movies onto CDs rather than DVDs, which is a useful option if you do not have a DVD writer.

- Windows Media Format

System requirements

In order to run Pinnacle Studio look for these minimum system requirements (or higher if possible):

- Pentium II or AMD Athlon 800 MHz processor or higher

- 256 MB RAM

- Windows 98 SE, ME, 2000 or XP (MicroMV support requires Windows XP)

- 500 MB of disc space to install software

For processing digital video the hard disc must be capable of sustained throughput of at least 4 MB/sec. (Most computers with a hard drive capacity suitable for storing digital video will also have the required processing power.)

- 120 MB of disc space for every 20 minutes of DV video captured at preview quality. Video footage can also be captured at a DVD quality setting which takes up considerably more hard disc space

- CD-ROM drive

- One free PCI slot for installing a FireWire card

- CD Writer (for creating VCDs or S-VCDs)

- DVD Writer (for creating DVDs)

Capture mode

Once Pinnacle Studio has been installed there are options for capturing, editing and publishing digital video. The first one that will be used is the capture mode:

There are different options for downloading digital and analog video. These are looked at in more detail in Chapter Two.

The video camera has to be turned on and connected to the computer before video can be captured.

Since the video camera controls can be accessed through Studio, the video camera does not have to be located right next to you.

Click here to access Capture mode

Downloaded video clips are displayed here

Video playback is displayed here

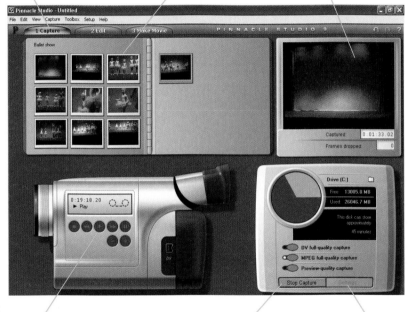

Video playback can be controlled here

Click here to start and stop downloading video footage from the video camera

Click here to access downloading settings

Edit mode

Once video footage has been downloaded in Capture mode, it can then be edited in Edit mode. This is the section in which your completed movie will be created:

Video editing tools

Click here to access Edit mode

Clip Player

The clip Player is the area where video clips and effects such as transitions and titles can be previewed. This can be done without adding the clips to a new movie project.

Click here to access video or audio toolboxes for a selected clip on the Timeline or Storyboard

Timeline or Storyboard for creating new movies. Video clips are added here

Movie Window area

Click here to change the Timeline or Storyboard views (and also text view)

Make Movie mode

The final step in the digital video process is publishing the completed movie into a suitable output format. This will vary depending on how you want to use the completed movie. For publishing with Pinnacle Studio the Make Movie mode is used:

Click here to select
an output option

Click here to access
Make Movie mode

When movies are being created in the selected format the process can take several hours depending on the length of the video footage. This is because Studio has to render the footage before it is saved. This involves processing all of the different elements in a movie so that it is ready to be created in the required format.

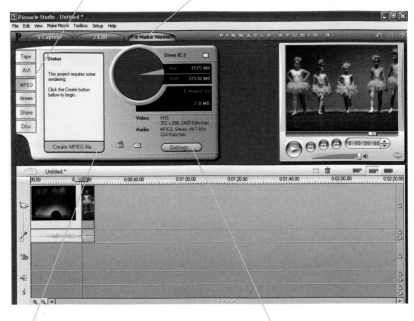

Click here to create a
movie in the selected
output format

Click here for settings
for the selected output
format

Capturing video

This chapter looks at how to connect video cameras to computers and some of the settings in Pinnacle Studio that are required for the downloading process.

Covers

Chapter Two

Connecting camera to computer

Once you have captured your video footage, the next step is to download it onto your computer so you can start editing it. The first part of this operation is to connect your camera to your computer and this varies depending on the type of footage that you have captured, e.g. digital or analog.

Connecting for digital footage

When digital video is recorded, a timecode is created on the tape. This is a counter that identifies a specific point on a tape and measures this in hours, minutes, seconds and frames. The timecode can then be used by Studio to locate sections of the tape. The timecode is created automatically when you record video, but if there is a break in recording then the continuous timecode will be broken. To ensure a continuous timecode, play the entire tape, with the lens cap on the camera, before you start using it. This will only record a blank movie, but it will create the timecode for the entire tape.

If you have captured digital video footage, you can connect your DV camera to a FireWire capture card with a FireWire cable.

Connect one end of the FireWire cable to the camera

Connect the other end to the computer's FireWire capture card

FireWire cards can be used to download a variety of digital data, not just digital video.

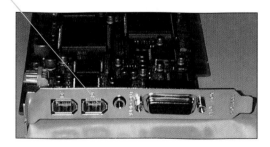

Connecting for analog footage

If you have captured analog video footage and you intend to convert it into digital footage on your computer you will need to do so through an analog to digital conversion device. These are either stand-alone units or they are capture cards that can be connected internally or externally to your computer.

Studio AV/DV Deluxe comes bundled with a break-out box (shown in the bottom image on this page) that can be used to download analog video.

Connect one end of the video and audio cables to the analog video camera

Connect the other end of the video and audio cables to the analog to digital conversion unit or video capture card

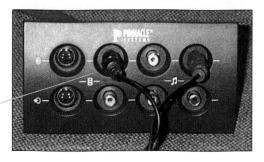

Capture interface

The Capture interface in Studio contains all of the elements required to download digital or analog video. It can be used to control the functions of a digital video camera and also download video at different quality settings.

Diskometer

One of the most important elements of the Capture interface is the Diskometer. This is where various settings can be applied for the video that is going to be captured. It also displays the amount of free disc space and the length of video that can be downloaded at a particular setting.

The Capture interface is displayed in full in Chapter One on page 14.

Amount of available disc space

Click here to select a different location for downloaded video

If you are going to be working with digital video a lot it would be worthwhile buying a new hard drive that can be used solely for this purpose. This could be either an internal or an external drive. If it is external, make sure it has a FireWire connection.

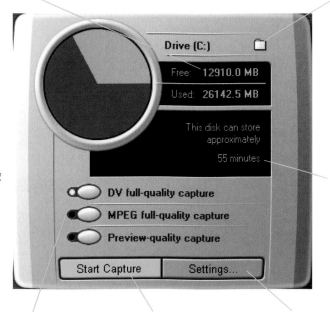

Amount of storage space for the selected quality option

Capture quality options

Click here to start downloading video

Click here for settings for the selected capture quality option

Capture settings

Once your camera has been connected to the computer you can specify the type of video to be downloaded and the format in which you want it transferred to your computer. There are different settings for capturing digital video and analog video:

DV settings

The DV full-quality capture setting produces the highest quality of video footage but creates very large file sizes as it is the video footage straight from the video camera without any additional compression. One hour of DV quality takes up approximately 13 GB of space on the hard drive. MPEG quality compresses the footage as it is taken from the camera and so produces smaller file sizes.

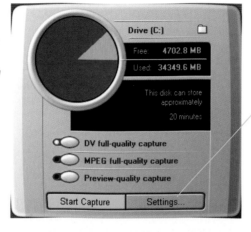

I Click the Capture tab and click the Settings button

2 Click the Capture Source tab and select a DV option under Video

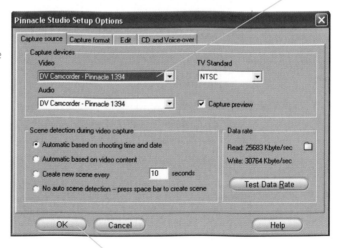

The source for the audio to be captured will be the same as the source for the video.

Click on the Test Data Rate button to ensure that your computer is capable of downloading video at a suitable speed.

3 Click the Capture Format tab and select a format option. Click OK to return to the main Capture menu

Analog settings

1 Click the Capture tab and click the Settings button

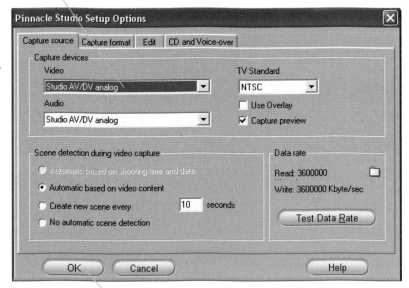

2 Click the Capture Source tab and select an analog option under Video

For analog video, settings can also be applied for the way the video is downloaded and for the associated audio.

3 Click the Capture Format tab and select a format option. Click OK to return to the main Capture menu

DV quality settings

SmartCapture

SmartCapture is a feature of Pinnacle Studio which allows you to download video footage in preview quality. The advantage of this is that it takes up considerably less disc space than the full-quality options. As a general rule, SmartCapture takes up approximately 10 times less disc space than the highest quality setting i.e. DV full-quality capture.

Once video has been downloaded using SmartCapture it can then be edited into a completed movie. When the movie is ready to be published, Studio can still produce it at DV full-quality. It does this by accessing the DV tape in the video camera and accessing the relevant parts of the tape that are required for the completed movie. To do this the camera has to be turned on and connected to the computer. When the movie is created it will be done so at full resolution. To use SmartCapture:

SmartCapture does not alter the quality of video when it is being edited. However, the original tape has to be accessed when the completed movie is being published.

1   Click here on the Diskometer

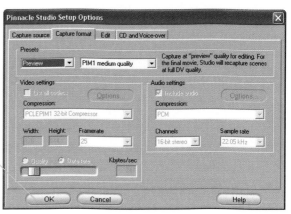

2   Click here to access the SmartCapture settings

3   Select the required settings and click OK

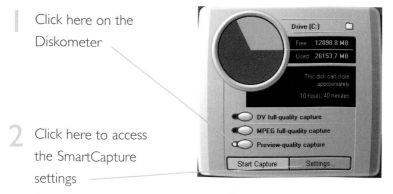

DV full-quality capture

This captures video at the highest available resolution, which results in the largest file sizes. The options for DV full-quality capture can be accessed in the same way as for SmartCapture.

For DV full-quality capture the default settings cannot be changed i.e. they are grayed-out

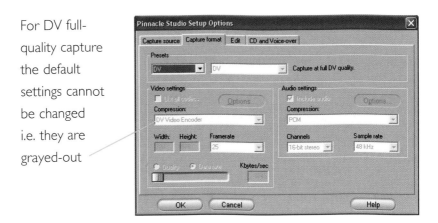

MPEG full-quality capture

For MPEG full-quality capture the options for publishing to DVD, S-VCD or VCD cannot be altered. If you want to edit the MPEG settings, select Custom in the Presets box to the right of the MPEG box.

This is the option that should be used for video that is going to be output on a DVD, S-VCD or VCD. However, if it is captured at another quality setting it can still be output to one of these formats from within Make Movie mode. The options for MPEG full-quality capture are accessed in the same way as for SmartCapture and DV full-quality capture.

Click here to select Custom options for the MPEG format

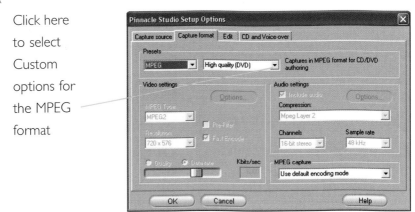

Scene detection

When downloading video (either digital or analog) onto your computer, the video editing software can automatically split it up into related clips. This is known as scene detection and it is a useful function for downloading video footage in manageable units rather than one long sequence. The scene detection settings are located within the Capture Source window:

Scene detection works by breaking up a single file into smaller units. However, these are still contained within the single file.

Access the scene detection options and specify how you want the scenes to be selected

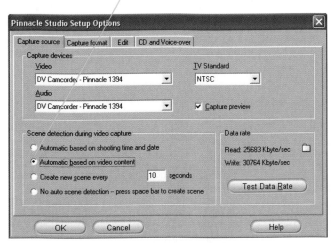

If you want to create scenes manually, this can be done by pressing the Space Bar at the appropriate moment during downloading.

If scene detection is used, the video will be downloaded in individual scenes rather than a continuous sequence

Downloading digital video

Once the video camera has been connected to the computer and the required settings selected, the video footage can then be downloaded. To do this:

1 Set the video camera controls to Play, VTR or VCR. Make sure it is not on Camera, Auto or Manual

When downloading video, use an external power adaptor with the video camera, rather than its removable battery.

2 Click the Capture tab to access the Capture window

3 Select the quality level for the video to be captured

Check the amount of free hard drive space before you start downloading video, to make sure there is enough for the amount of video you want to download.

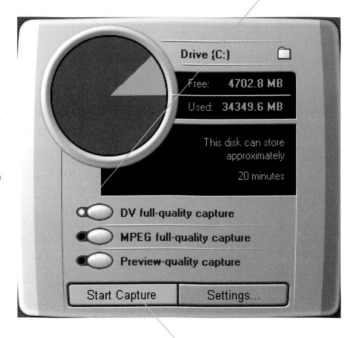

4 Click the Start Capture button

5 Enter a name for the footage that is going to be captured and click Start Capture

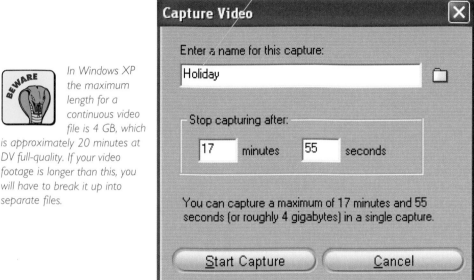

6 The camera controls can be activated from the Capture window, to cue to the correct point for capture

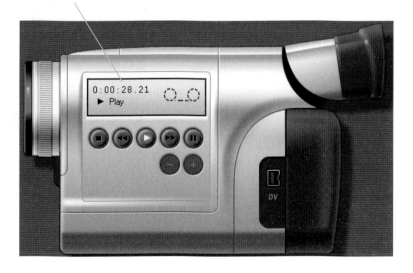

Downloading analog video

The basic process for downloading analog video is the same as for digital video, except that there are video and audio settings that can be applied before the Start Capture button is clicked.

1 Click here to select the type of analog video

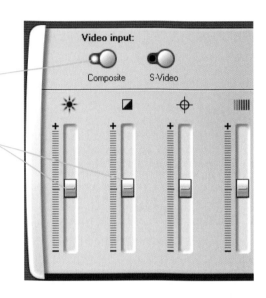

2 Drag these sliders to set options for the analog video to be downloaded. These are (from left to right) brightness, contrast, sharpness and color saturation

BEWARE

If an analog video camera is not connected then the analog downloading settings will not be available.

3 Click here to download audio with the video

4 Drag these sliders to set the audio levels

Pinnacle Studio interface

This chapter looks at some of the elements of the Pinnacle Studio interface, including the Album, the Menu bar and the Player. It also looks at creating and saving projects in Studio.

Covers

Chapter Three

The Album

The Album is the area where the majority of video editing takes place once the raw footage has been captured. This contains all of the necessary tools for creating a completed movie. These are:

- Video scenes. This option is used to access downloaded video footage

- Transitions. This option is used to add special effect transitions between video clips

- Titles. This option is used to add titles, either over an existing video clip or on a separate background

- Still images. This option is used to add still digital images or frame grabs from video footage

- Sound effects. This option is used to add sound effects

- Menus. This option is used to add interactive menus for navigation through the completed movie

The Album is an area for selecting and adding a lot of preset elements into a movie. For more control over the editing process use the Video and Audio toolboxes. For more information on these, see Chapter Four.

The available items for each Album option are displayed here

Video scenes

Transitions

Titles

Still images

Sound effects

Menus

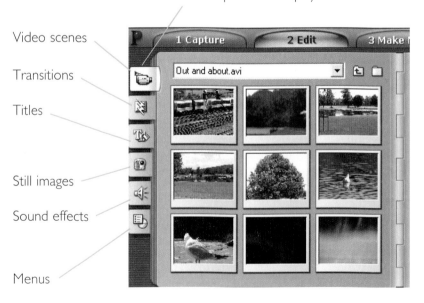

Click here to move backwards and
forwards through the available
pages for a particular Album item

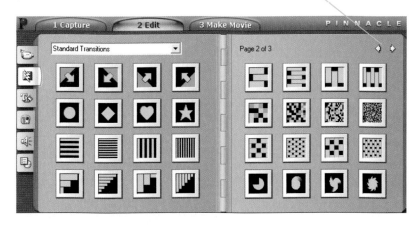

The clip Player can be used to preview video clips, transitions, titles, still images, sound effects and menus.

Click on an item in the Album to select it

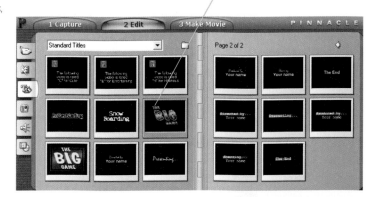

Most selected items can
be previewed in the clip
Player

Video scenes

Once video footage has been downloaded in Capture mode it can then be accessed through the video option in the Album. This just shows you the video scenes that are available. At this point they are not part of a new movie.

Click here to access the video option in the Album

Click here to access the available video files

 By default, captured video clips are downloaded into the Captured Video folder which is located within the main Pinnacle Studio folder. This is created when the program is installed.

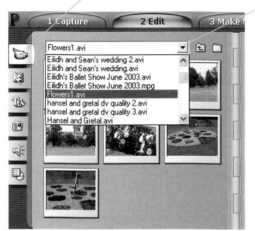

Once video scenes are added to the Storyboard or the Timeline, to create a movie, these are known as video clips.

Click here to access video files in a different location from the default one

The scenes within the selected video file are displayed within the Album and each scene can be previewed in the clip Player

Scene information

When video scenes are viewed in the Album it is possible to find out certain information about them by passing the cursor over a particular scene. The information displayed shows the start point of the scene, relative to the current sequence of video scenes, and the duration of the scene.

The duration of other items in the Album can also be displayed by passing the cursor over the required item.

Pass the cursor over a scene in the Album to view its start point and also its duration

The start point of a scene added to its duration should equal the start point of the next scene.

Viewing scenes

By default, scenes are displayed as icons. However, they can also be displayed with their details beside them. To do this:

1 Select View>Comment View from the Menu bar

The duration of video scenes is measured in hours, minutes, seconds and frames.

2 The details of each video scene are displayed here. This consists of the scene number and its duration

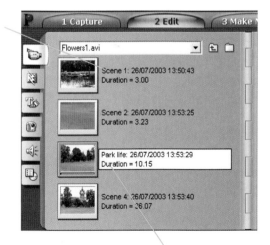

Once a scene has been given a unique name this can be used to locate similarly named scenes within the Album. To do this, select Album>Select Scenes by Name and then enter the search criteria. All of the scenes that match the search criteria keyword will be highlighted.

3 Click twice on a scene's details (this is two clicks with a short pause in between, rather than double-clicking) and overtype to give it a unique name

Combining scenes

Depending on how scene detection (if used) works during the downloading of video footage, you may want to combine video scenes within the Album. To do this:

1 Select two or more scenes (they have to be sequential)

To select sequential scenes in the Album, select the first scene, then Shift+click on the last scene in the sequence. To select non-sequential scenes, select the first scene, then Ctrl+click to select the rest of the scenes.

2 Select Album>Combine Scenes from the Menu bar

3 The selected scenes will be combined into a single one

Subdividing scenes

As well as combining scenes, it is also possible to subdivide scenes in the Album. To do this:

Scenes can also be split once they have been added to the Timeline. This allows for more precise editing than using the subdivide command.

1 Select a single scene

2 Select Album>Subdivide Scenes from the Menu bar

3 Enter a value for the length of each of the subdivided scenes. Click OK

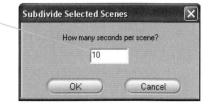

If scenes have been combined or subdivided it is still possible to restore them to their original state. To do this, first combine any scenes that have been subdivided. Then, select a scene that has been combined and select Album> Detect Scenes by Video Content (or Detect Scenes by Shooting Time and Date) from the Menu bar.

4 The scene is subdivided in the Album. The number of new scenes is dependant on the specified length for each scene, as defined in Step 3

Transitions

Transitions are special effects that can be inserted between scenes to smooth the change from one to another. Transitions work by overlapping between the end of one scene and the beginning of the next one. Transitions can be very simple, such as a basic fade in and fade out, or they can be quite dramatic and eye-catching.

Click here to access the transitions option in the Album

Click here to access the available transitions

Transitions should be used sparingly in movies, particularly the more flamboyant ones. Do not overuse them, otherwise their impact will be diminished.

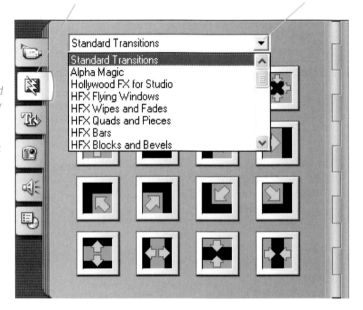

Select a transition and click here to preview the effect in the clip Player

Titles

Titles and text can be added to video clips in a variety of ways. Through the Album this is done with preset designs. These can be added to movies as titles on their own background. They can be edited, but only after they have been placed on the Timeline or the Storyboard of a new movie.

Additional titles can be accessed from Program Files>Pinnacle>Studio>Titles on the hard drive.

Click here to access the titles option in the Album

Click here to access additional titles on your hard drive

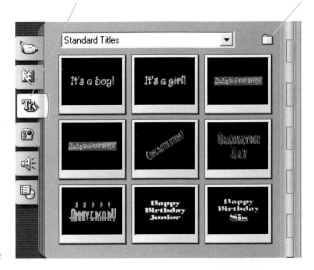

Titles have to be edited through the video toolbox once they have been added to the Timeline or the Storyboard.

Select a title and click here to preview its duration in the clip Player. Titles within the Album do not have any animated effects

Photos and frame grabs

Still images can be inserted between video clips, either in the form of digital photographs or frame grabs, which are still images taken from video footage. Still images can be used for a variety of reasons such as to emphasize a point within a movie or as a background for a title.

Frames of video footage can be grabbed in the video toolbox once a video clip has been added to the Timeline or the Storyboard. This is looked at in more detail in Chapter Ten.

Click here to access the photos and frame grabs option in the Album

Click here to access digital images from your own hard drive

Still images do not have to be photographic ones. Any graphical image can be used, such as an abstract design or a logo.

Select a photo or a frame grab to view it in the clip Player. Since it is a still image, there is no need to press the play button, as the image will not change for the duration of its length

Sound effects

Audio effects can be added to movies in a variety of ways: as sound effects, as background music or as a narration or voice-over. The sound effects are added through the Album, while the latter two are added using the audio toolbox.

Click here to access the sound
effects option in the Album

Click here to access sound
effects from a different
location on your hard drive

*Cover discs on
a lot of digital
video magazines
sometimes
contain a variety
of sound effects and these are
normally available free for users
to insert into their video projects.*

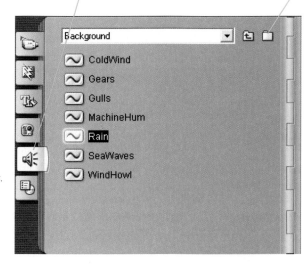

Select a sound effect and
click here to hear it in
the Player. Nothing
appears in the Player but
the sound will be heard if
the computer's speakers
are turned on

Menus

Menus can be added to movies that are going to be output to VCDs, S-VCDs or DVDs. They enable users to move between scenes and chapters of a movie by selecting one of the options on the menu. Usually, menus are inserted once a movie has been completed.

The menus created by Pinnacle Studio are similar in their functions to the menus used on commercial DVDs.

Click here to access the menu option in the Album

Click here to access menus from a different location on your hard drive

If a menu in the Album has a small yellow icon in the bottom right-hand corner, this indicates that the menu appears on an animated background. This can be previewed in the clip Player.

Select a menu and click here to view it in the clip Player

The Menu bar

The Menu bar contains menus that provide all of the functionality for the workings of Pinnacle Studio. Most of these commands can be accessed through other areas of the programs (such as the Album and the video and audio toolboxes) but they are located in one place on the Menu bar.

Click on an item on the Menu bar to see the related menu commands

The available menus on the Menu bar are:

- File. This contains commands for opening and saving existing video projects and also creating new ones

- Edit. This contains the standard cut, copy and paste commands and also commands for undoing previous operations and selecting and deleting items

- View. This is used to determine which part of the program is accessed. There are options for viewing the Capture, Edit and Make Movie modes. There are also options for viewing the Timeline, Storyboard or text view

- Album. This contains commands for accessing the elements of the Album and editing them accordingly, such as combining and subdividing video clips

- Toolbox. This contains commands for accessing the video and the audio toolboxes and the elements within them

- Setup. This contains commands for setup options for capturing video, formatting and editing it, capturing audio and also outputting completed video to different formats

- Help. This contains commands for the Studio help files and also online functions for product registration and information about updates to the program

The Player

The Player is the section of Studio that is used to preview a variety of elements. This is most frequently video clips, but it can also be used to preview transitions, titles, sound effects, menus and still images.

The Player can be used to preview items in the Album and also once they have been added to the Timeline or the Storyboard. If several items have been added to the Timeline or the Storyboard, they can all be previewed in sequence in the Player.

There are two versions of the Player. The default one is for standard video:

The Player is also available in the Capture window. This can be used to move to the required section of the tape before anything is captured and also to preview footage as it is being downloaded.

Preview window

Fast forward

Fast reverse

Scrubber – drag this to move through the clip

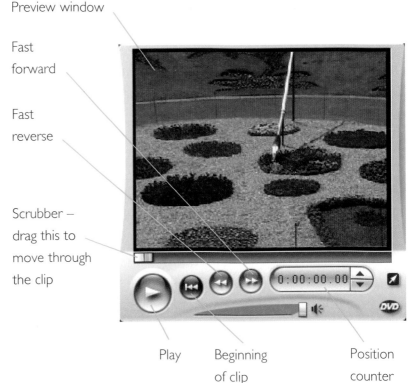

Play

Beginning of clip

Position counter

The second version of the Player is for previewing movies that are going to be published on DVDs, S-VCDs or VCDs. This version of the Player has controls that are similar to those on a commercial DVD player handset. These controls can be used to test the functionality of menus that have been added to a movie.

In DVD mode, any buttons that have been added to a menu can be selected and the corresponding operation will be applied on the Timeline.

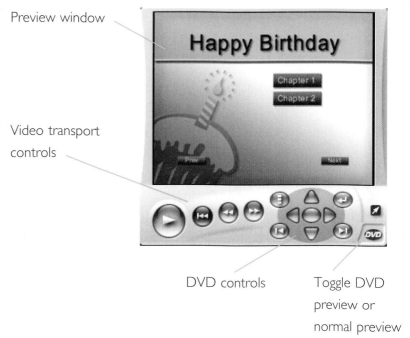

Preview window

Video transport controls

DVD controls

Toggle DVD preview or normal preview

DVD controls

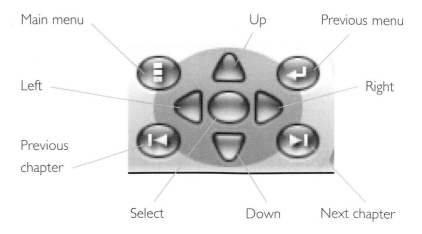

Main menu

Up

Previous menu

Left

Right

Previous chapter

Select

Down

Next chapter

The Storyboard

The Storyboard is one of three options for viewing video clips that have been used to create a new movie. Only the first scene of a video clip is displayed, but the whole clip can still be viewed in the Player. The Storyboard can also be used to display transitions, titles, still images and menus. However, it cannot be used to display sound effects. To use the Storyboard:

Video clips are shown
as single frames

Click here to access
Storyboard view

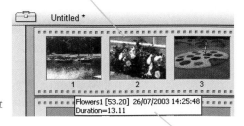

The Storyboard is a good way to get a quick overview of the elements in a movie. However, for greater editing flexibility, the Timeline is a better option (see next page).

Pass the cursor over a clip to display information about its start point and its duration

A variety of elements can be displayed on the Storyboard:

The elements on the Storyboard can be edited by accessing them in the video toolbox. For more information on this, see Chapter Four.

Overlay titles

Transitions

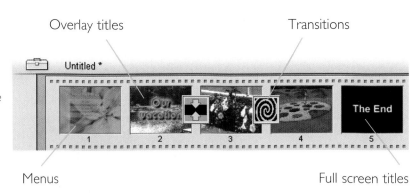

Menus

Full screen titles

The Timeline

The Timeline is the area of Pinnacle Studio where you will probably do most of your video editing. It displays all of the items in a movie and also their duration in relation to each other. The Timeline also displays a timescale, which shows the elements at any given point in the movie. To use the Timeline:

All of the viewing options are part of the Movie Window section of Pinnacle Studio.

The audio from the main video track is also known as synchronous audio.

Timescale bar

Click here to access the Timeline view

Video track

Audio from video track

Titles

Sound effects

Background music

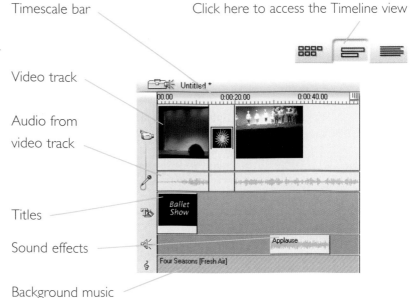

Drag here on the Timescale to enlarge or contract the scale. All of the elements on the Timeline are enlarged or contracted accordingly

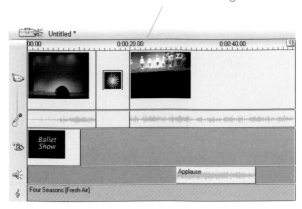

Text view

The third way for viewing information about items that have been added to a movie is Text view. This displays a chronological textual list of all of the elements of a movie. It also displays their duration and whether they have been trimmed or not. To use Text view:

Click here to access Text view

Sequence in which items appear in the movie

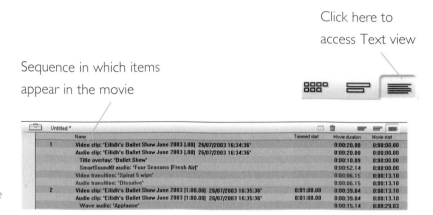

In Text view the Movie Duration column displays the duration of individual elements within a movie. The Movie Start column displays the aggregate duration of the entire movie.

Information about items is displayed here

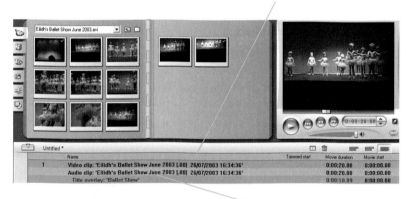

Click on an item to view it in the Player. If items are linked, i.e. a video clip and the synchronous audio, both items will be highlighted in Text view

Scrubber

The Scrubber is a tool that can be used to move to specific points in either video or audio clips. It appears in several areas of the Pinnacle Studio interface:

Player

The Scrubber is available in the Player in both Capture mode and Edit mode.

Drag here on the Scrubber in the Player to move through the item that is being displayed

Timeline

When the Scrubber is moved through a movie on the Timeline, the corresponding action is performed by the Scrubber in the Player.

Drag here on the Scrubber on the Timeline to move through a movie

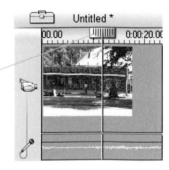

Toolboxes

Drag here on the Scrubber in the video or audio toolbox to move through the item that is being displayed

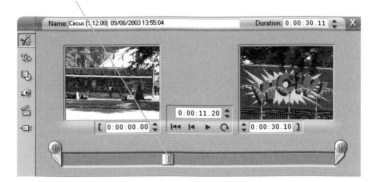

Pinnacle projects

Once movies have been created in Studio they are known as projects. There are a number of ways with which to work with them.

Saving projects

Projects can be saved into the proprietary Studio file format. This has a .stu extension and means that the files can subsequently be opened up in Studio again and edited further. To save projects:

Video files in non-proprietary formats, i.e. AVI and MPEG, cannot be opened in Pinnacle Studio for editing purposes.

1. Create a new movie and select File>Save Project from the Menu bar

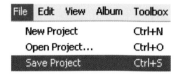

2. Navigate to a folder into which you want to save the project, give it a name and click Save

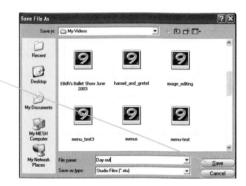

New Pinnacle projects can be created by selecting File> New Project from the Menu bar. However, only one project can be opened at any one time, so if a new one is opened, the current one is closed down. This is done with an option to save any changes that have been made to the project.

Opening projects

1. Select File>Open Project from the Menu bar

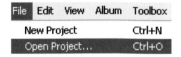

2. Navigate to a file you want to open and click Open

Toolboxes

The majority of video and audio editing takes place within the Pinnacle Studio toolboxes. This chapter shows how to access these toolboxes and looks at the items that can be edited and created within them.

Covers

Chapter Four

Video toolbox

The video toolbox is the area where the majority of video editing takes place. It can be used to edit existing items within a movie and it can also be used to add additional elements such as titles, menus, still images and special effects. The video toolbox can be accessed from either the Storyboard, the Timeline or Text view. When it is accessed, it opens in the appropriate mode for the item that is selected in the movie window.

Accessing the video toolbox

To access the video toolbox:

The video toolbox is used to edit clips that have been placed on either the Timeline or the Storyboard to create a new movie. If it is a video clip, the original video footage remains untouched and can still be added to a movie in its complete state.

2 Click here to open the video toolbox

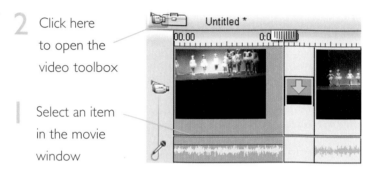

1 Select an item in the movie window

3 The video toolbox displays the selected item within the appropriate mode

The toolboxes can also be accessed by double-clicking on items on the Timeline or on the Storyboard.

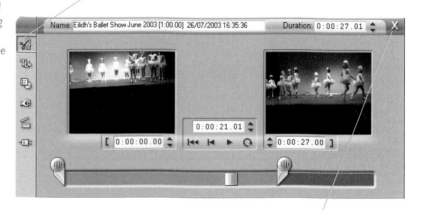

4 Click here to close the video toolbox

Video toolbox options

Depending on the item selected in the movie window, the video toolbox displays a different interface:

Video clips

Open a video clip and click here to display its properties   Video name   Duration box

If a video clip is played in the video toolbox, the preview is displayed in the Player, since the toolbox does not have the facility to play a continuous clip.

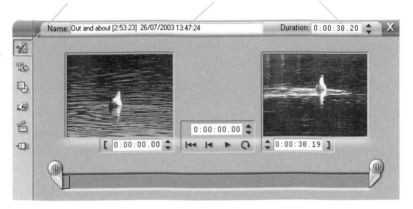

Transitions

Open a transition and click here to display its properties   Transition name   Duration box

The option to reverse the direction of a transition is not available for all of the transition effects.

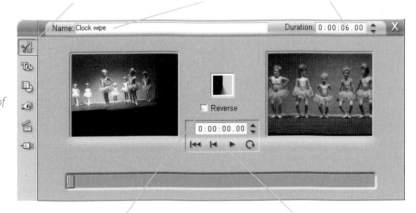

Check this box to reverse the transition   Playback controls

Titles

Open a title and click here
to display its properties

Title name

Duration box

The duration boxes within Pinnacle Studio display information in hours, minutes, seconds and frames.

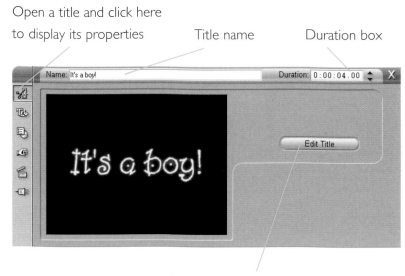

Click here to edit the title

Menus

For more information about creating and editing menus, see Chapter Eleven.

Open a menu and click here
to display its properties

Menu name

Duration box

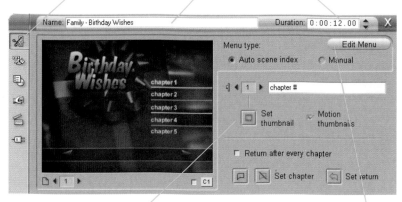

Use these options to edit
the functions of the menu

Click here to edit the
content of the menu

Video toolbox tools

There are a number of tools in the video toolbox that can be used for editing existing content in a movie and also adding new elements.

Clip properties

This option displays the properties of the selected item. For most items, it also allows for certain editing functions to be applied.

The clip properties option displays the properties for the type of clip selected. In the video toolbox this can include video clips, transitions, titles, sound effects and background audio.

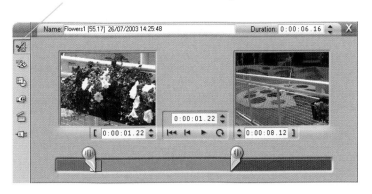

Titles

This option can be used to add titles to a movie:

Click on different items on the Timeline to have them appear in the video toolbox, without having to close the toolbox down first.

Click here to access the titles option

Click here to create overlay titles or full screen titles

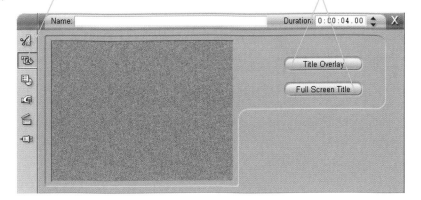

Menus

This option can be used to add menus to a movie at the point at which the video toolbox was accessed:

Click here to access
the menus option

Click here to create
a new menu

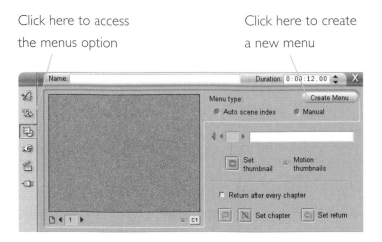

Frame Grab

This option can be used to capture single frames from existing video footage:

Click here to access the
frame grab option

Click here to select the source from
which the frame will be grabbed

If a frame is being grabbed from a video camera, the camera has to be connected to the computer and turned on.

Click here to grab frames

…cont'd

To create a
SmartMovie a
separate music
track is required,
in addition to the
audio recorded with the video.

SmartMovie

This option can be used to create polished music videos by selecting the video clips and the music and letting Studio do the rest:

Click here to access
the SmartMovie option

Click here to start the
SmartMovie process

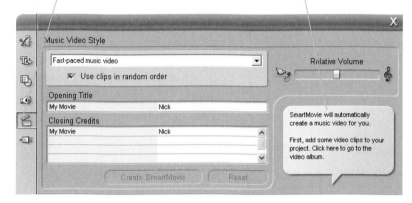

Video effects

This option can be used to add a variety of clean-up functions and special effects to video clips:

Video effects are
applied to an
entire video clip
once it has been
added to the
Timeline or the Storyboard.

Click here to access the
video effects option

Click here to select the
required video effects

Audio toolbox

The audio toolbox can be used to edit audio elements within a movie, or be used to add new audio elements. To use the audio toolbox:

2 Click here to open the audio toolbox

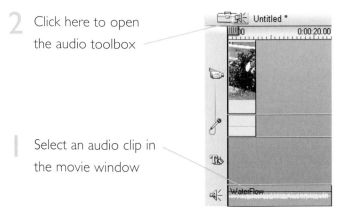

Select an audio clip in the movie window

Audio clips can be trimmed in the same way as trimming video clips. This involves trimming the clip and then creating Mark In and Mark Out points for the beginning and the end of the clip.

3 Click here to display the properties of the selected audio clip

The audio toolbox displays the length of each audio item, within the duration box at the top right corner of the toolbox.

4 Use these controls to edit the selected audio clip

5 Click here to close the audio toolbox and return to the Album

Audio toolbox options

The audio toolbox can be used to edit three different types of audio:

- Synchronous audio, which is the audio from the main video track

- Sound effects

- Background music

Each of these types of audio have slightly different options when they are accessed in the audio toolbox:

Synchronous audio
This is the audio that is recorded with the video footage.

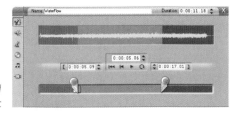

Narration and voice-overs are treated in the same way as sound effects and are included on this track.

Sound effects

Sound effects and background music operate in a similar way when they are added to a movie. However, the synchronous audio is more unique as it is linked to the recorded video.

Background music

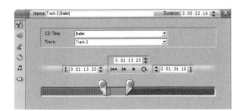

Audio toolbox tools

In addition to using the clip properties option in the audio toolbox for editing existing audio elements, there are also various other tools that can be used to edit and create audio elements.

Volume

Click here to access the volume option

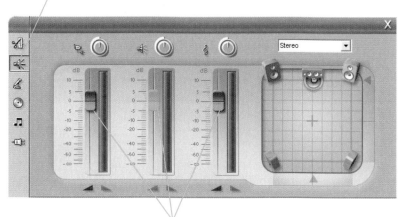

The volume controls can be used so that all three audio tracks can be used within the same movie. To do this, adjust the volume of each track accordingly.

Drag these sliders to change the volume of different audio tracks

Balance

The balance of an audio track i.e. the speaker from where the audio is played, can also be adjusted within the volume option:

The surround sound balance option can be used when publishing movies that will be viewed on a home cinema system i.e. one with more than two speakers.

Drag the audio track icons to alter the balance for either stereo or surround sound systems

Narration

Click here to access the narration option

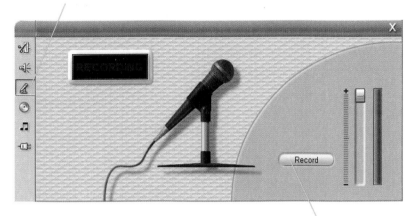

Click here to start recording a narration or voice-over

Add background music

Click here to access the add background music option

Select an audio track here from a CD

If background music is being added from a CD, the CD has to remain in the CD drive until after it has been added to the movie.

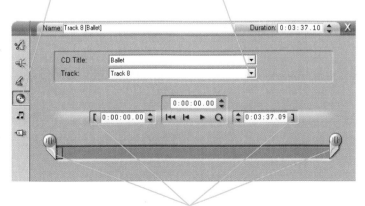

Edit the background music using these controls

SmartSound

SmartSound is an option that is unique to Pinnacle Studio and it can be used to add background music automatically to a movie.

Click here to access the add SmartSound option

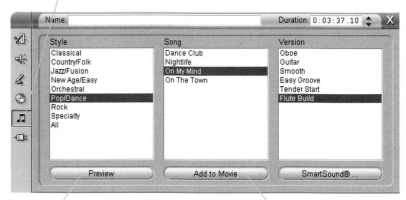

Click here to preview a music effect

Click here to add the music to the current movie

Audio effects

Click here to access the audio effects option

Click here to select the required audio effects

Audio effects can be added to any type of audio within a movie i.e. audio captured with a video clip, sound effects, music and narration.

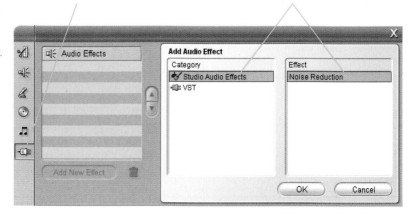

Adding clips

Adding clips to the Timeline

Clips can be added to either the Timeline or the Storyboard by dragging them from where they are located in the Album. On the Timeline, different types of clips are added to different parts of the Timeline:

The term "clips" refers to any content that is added to a movie. It can cover video clips, sound clips, transition clips, title clips and menu clips.

Drag a clip from the Album and place it on the associated track on the Timeline. A green tick appears on any video clips that have been added to the Timeline

Sound clips can only be added to the Timeline, not the Storyboard.

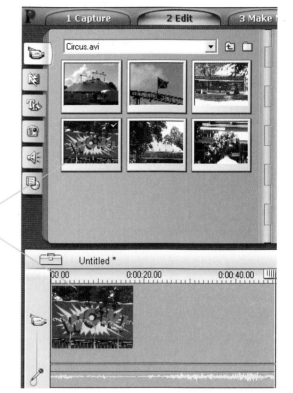

If you try and add a clip to the wrong place on the Timeline, i.e. a video clip onto the titles track, a red border will appear and you will not be able to place the clip

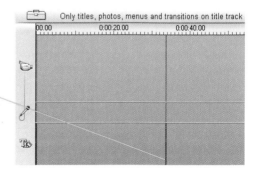

Adding clips to the Storyboard

Clips can be added to the Storyboard in the same way as the Timeline, by dragging them from their respective Albums:

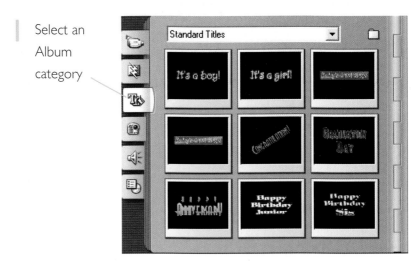

1 Select an Album category

Clips can also be added to Text view, but since this does not afford a graphical display, it is not the best option when first adding clips to a movie.

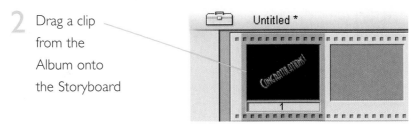

2 Drag a clip from the Album onto the Storyboard

To see the duration of a clip on the Storyboard, pass the cursor over the clip until a popup box appears.

3 Each clip is displayed in an individual container on the Storyboard (except transitions, which are located between two video clips)

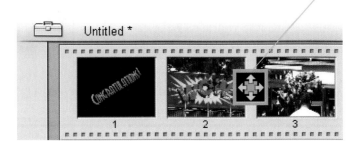

Adding clips from different files

It is possible to add video clips to movies from several different files that have been downloaded. To do this:

Click here to access the video clips in the Album

It is also possible to add sound effects and still images from different locations on your hard drive.

Drag a video clip onto the Timeline

Click here to access another video file from which clips can be added to the current movie

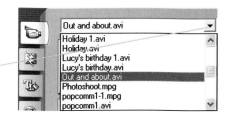

Click here to browse your hard drive for video files in other locations

Selecting clips

Once clips have been added to the Timeline or the Storyboard it is important to be able to select individual clips so that they can be previewed in the Player or have editing effects applied to them in the video or audio toolboxes. To do this:

1 Click once on a clip to preview it in the Player

If non-sequential video clips are selected on the Timeline or the Storyboard, the whole movie will still be previewed in the Player i.e. the selected clips will not play independently from the rest of the movie.

2 Click on a clip and click here to open it in the appropriate toolbox

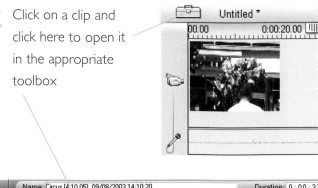

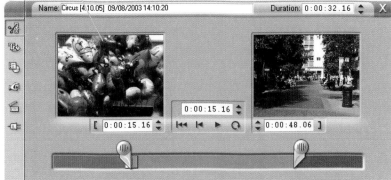

Moving clips

Some types of clips can be moved to different locations within a movie and this should be done on the Timeline.

Click and drag a clip to move it to a different point on the Timeline

Video clips cannot be moved if this causes a break in the movie i.e. there would be no content at a certain point if the clip were moved.

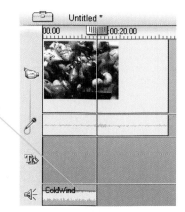

This will affect the point at which it occurs in the movie

Clips can be moved by selecting them on the Timeline or the Storyboard and selecting the Edit>Cut command from the Menu bar. Move to where you want to move the clip and select Edit>Paste from the Menu bar.

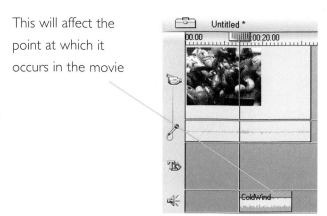

If it is not possible to move a certain item, a red border will appear when you try and move it to a new location

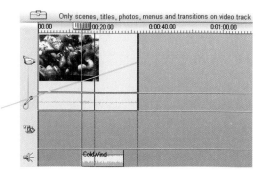

Rearranging and deleting clips

Once clips have been added to the Storyboard or Timeline it is possible to rearrange the order in which they play or delete them from a project.

Rearranging

1 Click and drag a clip on the Storyboard or the Timeline

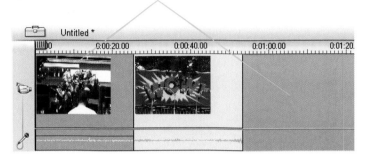

2 Place it at a different point to rearrange it

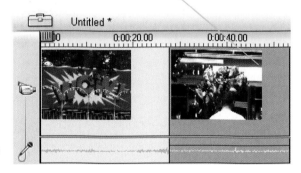

Once a clip has been deleted from a movie, it can be reinstated by dragging it from the Album. The clip is only removed from the current movie, not from the Album.

Deleting

Right click on a clip and select Delete from the menu, or click on the wastebasket icon

Trimming clips

Trimming individual clips is one of the fundamentals of digital video editing, as it allows you to remove unwanted parts of your captured footage. The two main techniques that are used are setting a clip's beginning and ending points and also splitting clips. This can be done in the video toolbox or on the Timeline:

Trimming clips with the video toolbox

Drag a clip onto the Storyboard or Timeline

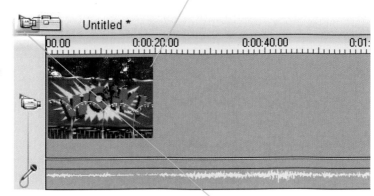

Trimming a clip once it has been added to a movie does not affect the original clip in the Album.

Clips that have been trimmed, or combined, can be reset to their original state by selecting Edit>Undo from the Menu bar or by deleting the clip from the Timeline or the Storyboard and then reinserting it from the Album.

2 Double click on the clip, or click here, to open the video toolbox

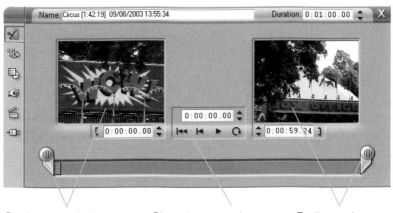

Beginning point   Play clip controls   Ending point

3 Drag the Scrubber to where you want the clip to begin

Use the duration timers in the video toolbox for precise editing of a clip. If values are entered into the timer boxes, the clips are trimmed at these points. Keep an eye on the timers as the clip is being played so that you know the exact point at which you want to trim a clip.

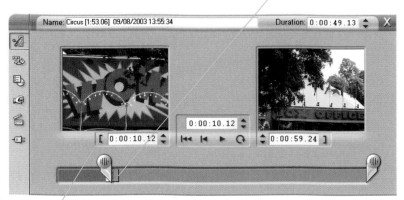

4 Click here to set the Mark In point

5 Repeat for the Mark Out point of the clip

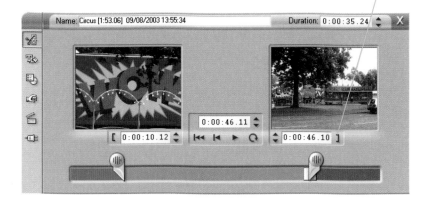

6 The edited clip is displayed on the Storyboard or the Timeline

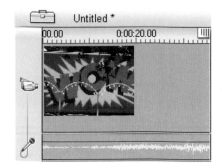

...cont'd

Trimming clips with the Timeline

1   Original clip

When the cursor is placed over the border of a clip, a single- or double-headed arrow appears. This indicates the direction in which the clip can be trimmed.

2   Click and drag here on the Timeline to trim the ending point

Video clips cannot be trimmed on the Storyboard. However, the clip editing function in the video toolbox can be accessed when in Storyboard mode. To do this, double click on a video clip on the Storyboard.

3   Click and drag here on the Timeline to trim the beginning point

4   As the clip is being trimmed, the corresponding actions are applied automatically in the video toolbox

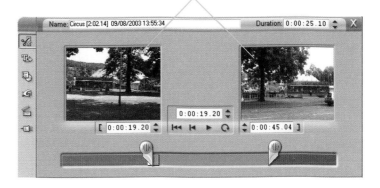

Splitting clips

In a lot of instances it is useful to be able to split a clip so that other elements can be inserted. This could include a textual title that conveys information about the action in the video, a still image or another video clip. When a clip is split it is actually duplicated and each new clip is trimmed at the appropriate points to create two new clips with a break in between them. Clips can be split on either the Storyboard or on the Timeline.

Splitting clips on the Storyboard

If you are going to be using transitions either before or after a split clip, make sure the clip is not too short, otherwise the transition may not operate properly.

1 Select a clip on the Storyboard

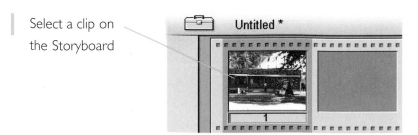

2 In the Player, drag the Scrubber to the point at which you want to split the clip

The duration timer box in the Player shows the exact point at which a clip will be split.

3 Click the Split Clip button

4 The original clip is split in two on the Storyboard

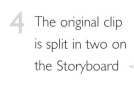
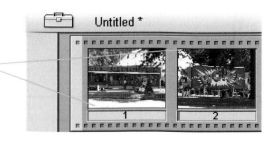

Splitting clips on the Timeline

Select a clip on the Timeline

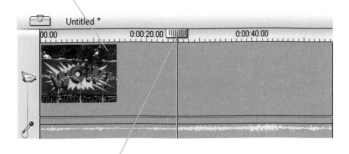

2 Drag the Scrubber to the point in the clip at which you want to split it

3 Click the Split Clip button

4 The original clip is split in two on the Timeline

5 Once a clip has been split, access the video toolbox to see how the split has affected the trimming of each individual clip

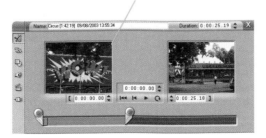

Combining clips

It is possible to combine clips that have been added to the Timeline or the Storyboard. To do this:

If two clips on the Timeline are allowed to be combined, there will be a dotted line between them.

1 Select two or more clips on the Timeline or on the Storyboard. They must be sequential in the Album

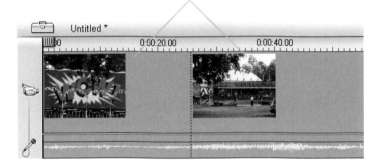

Clips can only be combined if the first one has not already been trimmed. However, it is still possible to combine them if the second one has been trimmed.

2 Right click on one of the selected clips

3 Select Combine clips from the menu

Clip Properties	
Go to Title/Menu Editor	
Play	Spacebar
Delete	Delete
Cut	Ctrl+X
Copy	Ctrl+C
Paste	Ctrl+V
Split clip	Insert
Combine clips	
Find Scene in Album	

Clips have to be in sequence on the Timeline or on the Storyboard in order for them to be combined into a single clip.

4 The selected clips are combined into a single one

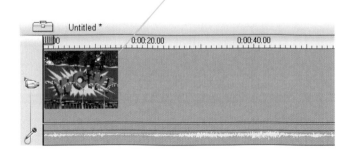

Locking the Timeline

When working with clips on the Timeline it is sometimes useful to be able to lock specific tracks. This means that the items on that track cannot be accessed or edited. Other tracks can then be edited, without any of the changes having an impact on the locked tracks. To lock tracks on the Timeline:

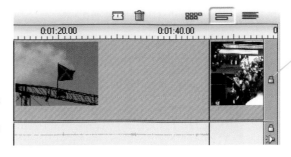

To unlock a track that has been locked, click once on the red padlock icon.

Click here to lock a track. This is denoted by a red padlock icon

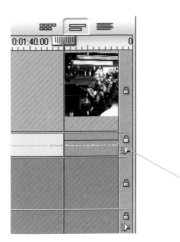

Numerous tracks can be locked, if required. The locked tracks are grayed out. The unlocked tracks are blue when selected

Once a track has been locked, it is not possible to select any items on that track or perform any editing tasks

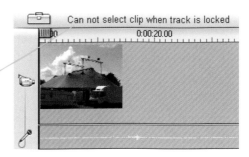

Insert editing

In addition to the basic clip editing tasks of splitting and combining video clips, it is also possible to perform more advanced editing techniques. One of these is the insert edit. This involves inserting a clip within a video clip, while the original audio track plays for the duration of both elements. This can be useful if you want to include something like a cutaway shot into a video, while still having a continuous commentary. To create an insert edit:

Before performing an insert edit, play the video clip through and make a note of the points at which you want to split the clip for editing purposes.

1   Click here to lock the synchronous audio track

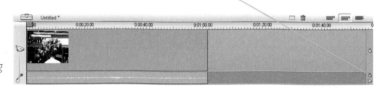

2   Drag the Scrubber to the point at which you want the inserted video clip to begin. Click here to split the clip

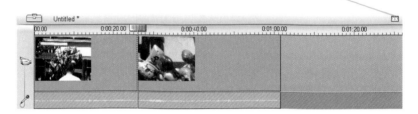

3   Drag the Scrubber to the point at which you want the inserted video clip to end. Click here to split the clip

4 Select the middle clip and click here to delete it from
the Timeline

5 A gap is created on the main video track where a portion
of the video has been deleted. The synchronous track is still
completely intact

*If nothing is
added to the gap
on the video track
the soundtrack
will keep playing
at this point, but the screen will
freeze at the last frame of the
previous video clip.*

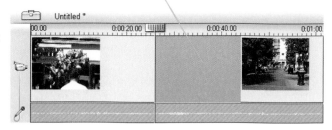

6 Drag a video clip, or still image, into the gap on the main video
track. If it is a video clip and longer than the available space
then it will automatically be trimmed to fit

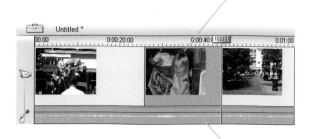

7 When the synchronous audio track is unlocked the original
audio track plays for the entire length of all of the clips on the
video track

Split editing

A similar technique to insert editing is split editing. This is when the video track or an audio track overlaps the preceding or succeeding clip. This can be used to fade in or fade out video or audio into the next clip. There are two types of split editing that can be performed. These are the "L-cut" and the "J-cut" split edits.

L-cut split editing

When performing split edits, run both of the video clips through and make a note of the points at which you want the edits to occur, if they are not at the beginning and end of the clips. Once they are added to the Timeline, trim them at these points.

1 Add two video clips to the Timeline. Trim them for the amount you want the edit to overlap each clip

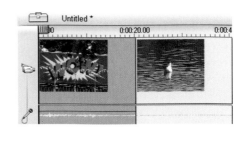

2 Click here to lock the video track

3 Drag the synchronous audio track to the right so that it stretches underneath the second video clip

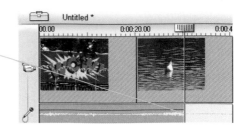

4 Unlock the video track. The audio from the first video clip will now continue playing for the specified amount of the second video clip

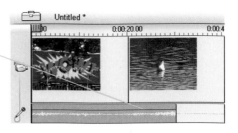

J-cut split editing

1 Add two video clips to the Timeline. Trim them for the amount you want the edit to overlap each clip

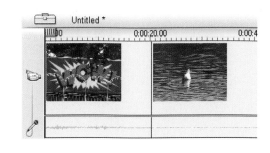

2 Click here to lock the audio track

A J-cut split edit could be used if you have some audio at the end of one track that you do not want. As long as the audio in the next clip is appropriate, this can be used using a J-cut.

3 Drag the border of the first video clip to the right so that it stretches over the audio track below it

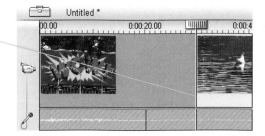

4 Unlock the audio track. The audio from the second clip will now start playing before the first video clip has finished playing

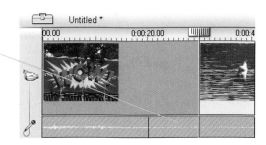

SmartMovie

SmartMovie is a function that can compile completed movies automatically. All that you need to do is specify the video clips and music you want to use and some of the settings. SmartMovie then creates the whole movie. The final version is in the form of a music video, with the selected music playing in addition to the audio that is recorded with the video. To use SmartMovie:

1 Open the video toolbox and click here

The Relative Volume slider can be used to alter the balance between the audio recorded with the video and the music that is added by SmartMovie.

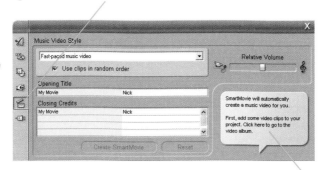

2 Click here to add video clips

3 Add video clips and click here to return to SmartMovie

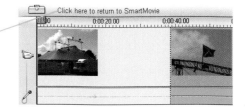

For SmartMovie to work effectively, the length of the video clip, or clips, should be longer than the length of the music that is added.

4 Click here to select music for the SmartMovie

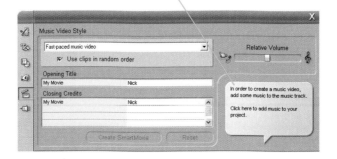

5 Select an option for adding music and click OK. Select the music according to this option

6 Click here to select a style for the selected music

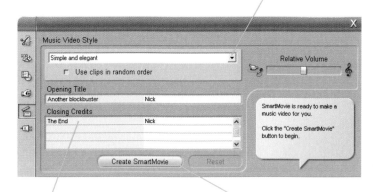

The elements of a SmartMovie, such as titles and transitions, can still be edited once the movie has been created and completed.

7 Enter details for the opening and closing credits

8 Click here to create the SmartMovie

9 The movie is created, including transitions and titles. The music is edited to match the length of the movie

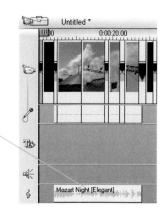

Video effects

Studio contains a variety of video effects which can be added to individual clips. These effects range from ones that can be used to enhance the appearance of a clip (such as color correction) to fun effects (such as lens flare). To add video effects:

1 Open a video clip in the video toolbox and click here

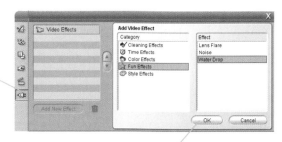

The Time Effects category contains options for speeding up and slowing down video clips.

2 Select a category and an effect and click OK

3 Select the attributes for the effect and click here to add it to the clip

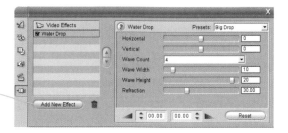

Color and visual effects are effective when applied to short video clips. Otherwise they can be too overpowering.

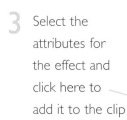

4 The effect can be viewed in the Player or in the final published movie

5 On the Timeline, effects are not visible but are denoted by the relevant icons under the clip

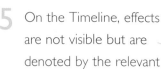

Transitions

This chapter looks at the types of transition effects that can be used between two video clips. It shows how to add them to a movie, edit them and how to create some basic special effects.

Covers

Chapter Six

About transitions

Transitions are a common device for blending the break from one video clip into another. This serves to make the transition smoother rather than a sudden break between clips.

Transitions are placed between two existing video clips that have been added to the Storyboard or the Timeline to create a new movie project. The transition then interacts with each of the clips in a variety of ways, depending on the type of clip being used.

1 The first clip plays normally until the transition begins to take effect

HOT TIP *One of the most effective transitions is a simple fade from one clip to another. If you are using transitions frequently, this is one that you should always keep in mind as it is subtle and professional.*

2 At the point where the transition is inserted, the effect begins to play between the two clips, merging them together

3 Once the transition is completed the second clip plays normally

Accessing transitions

Pinnacle Studio has a wide range of transitions that can be added to movie clips. To access these:

1 Click here on the Album to access the available transitions

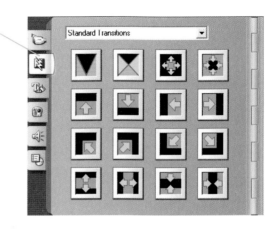

Transitions can be previewed in the Player. It is better to preview the transition effect in the Album first, before it is added to a movie. This is because the transition in the Album generally gives a clearer impression of how the effect works.

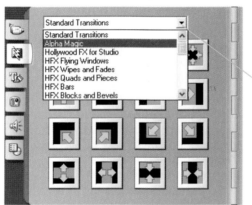

2 Click here to select different transition files within the transitions folder

3 The transitions category is displayed here

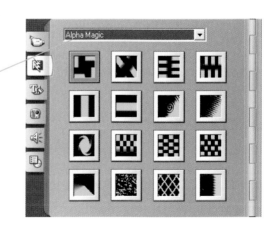

Fade in or out transitions

The most basic, and frequently the most effective, type of transition is one that causes the first video clip to fade out and the second one to fade in:

In a lot of cases it is just as effective to use no transitions in a movie. A lot of television programs do not use many transitions as they are more suited to home movies.

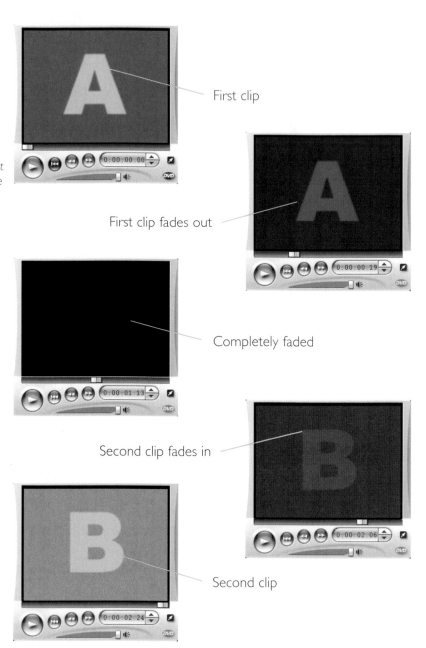

First clip

First clip fades out

Completely faded

Second clip fades in

Second clip

Standard transitions examples

Top left corner wipe

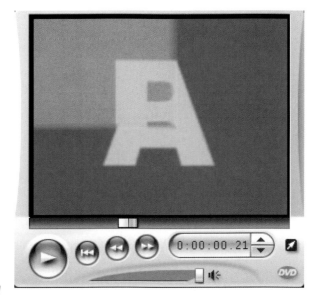

Try and use an appropriate transition for the video footage being used. For example, a corporate video could use fairly simple transitions, while a vacation video could use more varied and exciting transitions.

Star wipe

Matrix wipe

The Matrix wipe can be used to create a snowy effect which can be used for the disappearing effect shown on page 99.

Pinwheel wipe

Alpha Magic examples

The Alpha Magic examples that are included with Pinnacle Studio offer more advanced effects than the standard transitions:

BlackHole

As a general rule, the more complex the transition effect, the more sparingly it should be used.

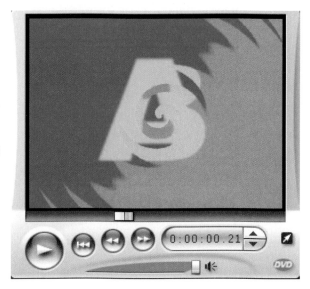

Flag

Glass

MorningStar

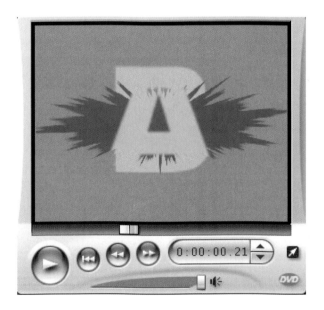

Hollywood FX examples

The Hollywood FX transitions are a group of third-party effects that are included with Pinnacle Studio. There are 16 Hollywood FX transitions that can be used with video clips. There are also examples of other Hollywood FX transitions that can be bought separately.

1 Click here to access the Hollywood FX transitions that can be used with video clips in Pinnacle Studio

Pro and Plus Pro transitions can be added to the Timeline or the Storyboard, but they still retain their respective watermarks.

2 Other Hollywood FX transitions can be previewed here. These are denoted by a Pro or a Plus Pro watermark

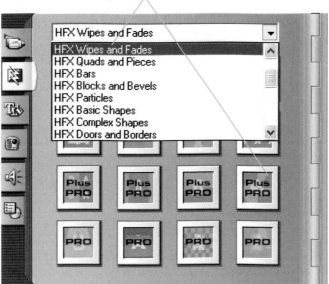

Mini balls chaos

Gem stone

Obtaining more transitions

More Hollywood FX transitions can be bought online from the Pinnacle website. To do this:

1 Open one of the Hollywood FX transition files

You have to register your version of Pinnacle Studio before you can access the related online resources. If you do not do this when you first instal the program it can be done by selecting Help>Product Registration from the Menu bar from within Pinnacle Studio.

2 Click here to access the Pinnacle website

3 Enter your login details to access the online resources for Pinnacle products and related plug-ins

If you forget your login details, there is a link on the login page which can be used to have your details emailed to you.

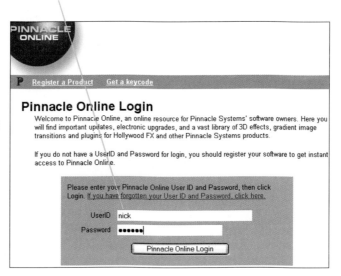

4 Select the required product and click here to buy it

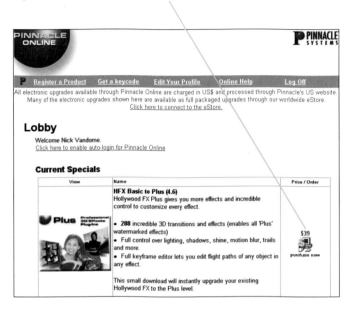

5 Once a Hollywood FX product has been purchased the watermarks are removed from the relevant items and the transitions can be used in movies

For Pro and Plus Pro transitions, the transitions editor can be assessed from the Edit button in the transitions panel of the video toolbox. This button is only available for Pro and Plus Pro transitions.

6 Hollywood Pro and Plus Pro transitions have their own editor

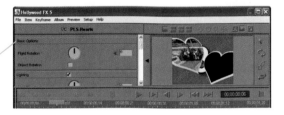

Adding transitions

Transitions are added by dragging them between two existing video clips on the Storyboard or the Timeline.

1 Click here to access the transitions

The length of a transition affects the amount that is played of the proceeding and succeeding video clips. So if a transition is lengthened, less of the video clips will be visible.

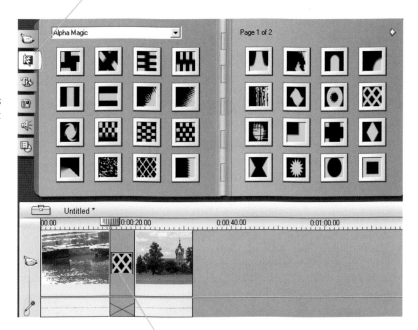

2 Drag a transition between two existing video clips on the Storyboard or the Timeline

3 Preview the transition effect in the Player

Editing transitions

Transitions can be edited on the Timeline and also in the clip properties section of the video toolbox:

Editing with the Timeline

1 Drag a transition onto the Timeline and select it by clicking on it once

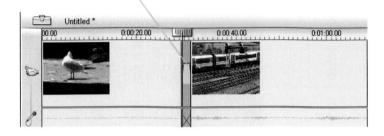

Either of a transition's borders can be dragged to edit its length. Whichever side is dragged, both video clips are updated accordingly, to take into account the new length of the transition.

2 Drag on one of the borders to alter the length of the transition

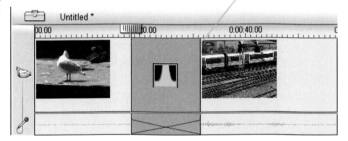

3 Preview the transition effect and its timing in the Player

...cont'd

Editing with the video toolbox

1   Double-click on a transition on the Timeline to open it in the video toolbox

By default, transitions are 1 second and 24 frames in duration.

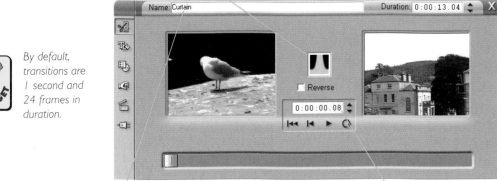

When a transition is given a custom name this only applies to the specific transition at that point in a movie. The custom transition is not available from the transition files.

2   Select the name of the transition and overtype to give it a custom name

3   Edit the duration of the transition by entering a new value here

4   If the option is available, check this box to reverse the transition effect

Special effects with transitions

Transitions are a good way to add some creativity into your movie making, not just with the transition effects themselves, but also with effects that can be created with adjacent video clips.

Making someone disappear

A very simple but effective video editing trick is to make a person or an object disappear before the viewers' eyes. To do this:

1   Create a video clip of someone, or something, against a plain background

When capturing a plain background for an example like the one on this page, the exposure of the clip may be different from the one with someone standing in front of it (for the plain background the exposure is taken from the background and in the other shot the exposure is taken from the individual or object). If this happens, lighten or darken the color of the background clip within the color effects window in the video toolbox.

2   Add the video clip to the Timeline

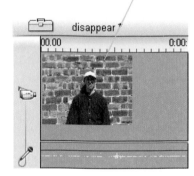

3   Create another video clip, this time of just the plain background

4   Add the video clip to the Timeline, after the first clip

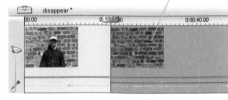

5 Select a transition such as vertical bars or a snowy effect

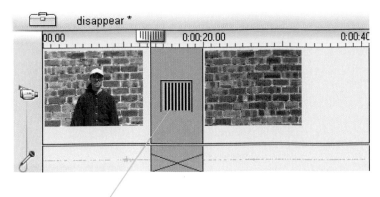

Include a recognizable feature in the background, such as a picture or a textured background. This will give more definition to the background and make the disappearing effect more dramatic.

6 Drag the transition between the video clips

7 When the video is played, it appears as if the person or object is vanishing into thin air

The perfect wedding

Wedding videos can be given an extra dimension by the constructive use of transitions:

Create a romantic effect with a heart-shaped transition

Use a matrix transition followed by a plain white background to create the impression of confetti

Title Editor

Titles are an integral part of creating professional-looking movies with Pinnacle Studio. These are created within the Title Editor. This chapter looks at how to access the Title Editor and how to create, edit and manipulate textual elements within it.

Covers

Chapter Seven

Accessing the Title Editor

The area in which titles and textual elements are added is known as the Title Editor. This can be accessed in a variety of ways:

- Select a video clip on the Timeline or the Storyboard and access the video toolbox. Then click here to access the Title Editor options

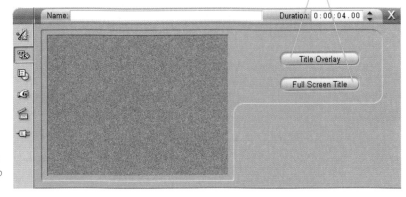

If no title has been added to a movie the initial window in the Title Editor is blank. If a title has already been added, then it can be opened up directly in the Title Editor.

- Double click on an existing title on the Timeline or the Storyboard

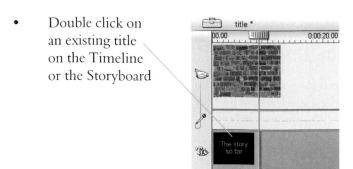

- Right click on a clip on the Timeline or the Storyboard and select Go to Title/Menu Editor from the contextual menu

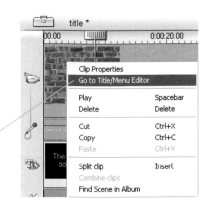

Functions of the Title Editor

Title Editor interface

The Title Editor is the area in which titles and interactive disc menus can be created:

Titles can be created either with, or without, graphical backgrounds.

Title type buttons   Text formatting   Font, background and button options

Editing window   Manipulation tools   Text styles

Title type buttons

The title type buttons determine the format in which the title is created. Click on one to select the required format:

   Static title

   Scroll up

   Crawl from right to left

Menu buttons

Manipulation tools

The manipulation tools can be used to perform a variety of tasks within the Title Editor:

 Selection tool

 Add text box tool

 Add ellipse tool

 Add rectangle tool

 Move, scale and rotate tool

 Kern and skew tool

 Group tool

 Ungroup tool

The Align tool brings up a menu with various alignment options. The Justify tool brings up a grid containing various options for justifying text.

 Align tool

 Justify tool

 Cut tool

 Copy tool

Paste tool

Delete tool

Selecting text boxes

Text boxes are one of the most important elements of a title and it is possible to select them in different ways:

Inserting the cursor within a text box. To do this, click on the selection tool and click anywhere within the text box

For the purpose of moving text boxes, they can also be selected by pressing Ctrl+A on the keyboard.

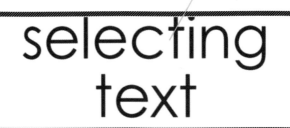

Selecting text within a text box. To do this, click on the selection tool and drag within the text box

Selected parts of text within a text box appear on a solid background.

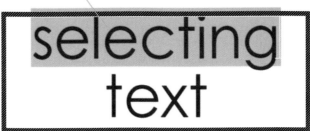

Activating the control points. To do this, click on the selection tool and click on the border of the text box. The control points should appear. These can be used to move and manipulate the text box

If the border of a text box is not visible, click once within the text box with the selection tool to activate the border. Then click on the border to activate the control points.

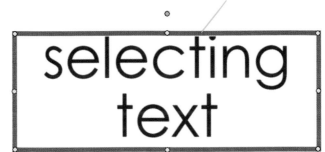

Adding text

To add text in the Title Editor:

1 Select the text tool

2 Click in the editing window and begin typing. This creates a text box which expands as far as the red border in the Title Editor

An expanding text box begins at the point at which the cursor is inserted within the Title Editor window.

or

Drag the text tool in the editing window. This creates a text box of a set width. The text will wrap downwards as you type

A sized text box should be large enough to accommodate the boxes largest word in its entirety. Otherwise the letters within the word will appear on different lines.

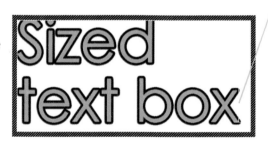

3 The text is formatted according to the formatting options that are selected here

Moving text

Once text has been added it can be moved or rotated. To do this:

1 Using the selection tool, click on a text box border to access the control points

Do not move too much text away from the horizontal. This makes it harder to read and can be annoying for people viewing the published video.

2 Drag here to rotate the text box

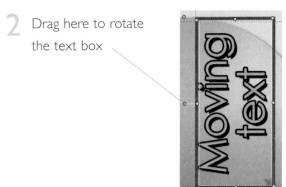

3 Drag anywhere on the border to move the text box

Formatting text

Text that is being used for titles can be formatted in a variety of ways. To format text once it has been added as a title:

Preset styles can be applied to a text box, by activating the box's control points and clicking once on a new style.

Click on a text box in the Editing title window

Click here to select a font

Click here to select a text size

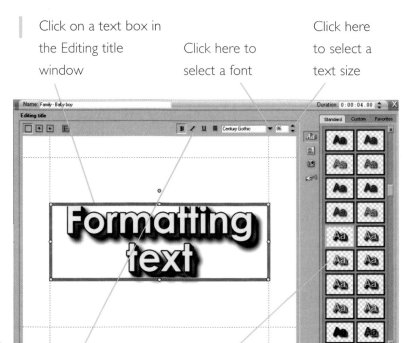

Try to limit the use of underlining with text as this makes it harder to read, particularly if the letters are all in capitals. To add emphasis to a word, use bold or italics instead.

Click here to select Bold, Italic, Underline and Justify formatting

Click here apply a preset style

2 The formatting is displayed in the Title Editor. Click OK to apply the title

Custom formatting

Custom formatting can be used to create your own text styles which can be applied to the currently selected text box. To do this:

1 Highlight text, or select the text box, in the Title Editor window

Depending on the format in which a video is saved, the quality of text can deteriorate in the published movie.

2 Click on the Custom tab

3 Select the colors of the text face i.e. the main surface of the text and also the amount of blur that is required, if any

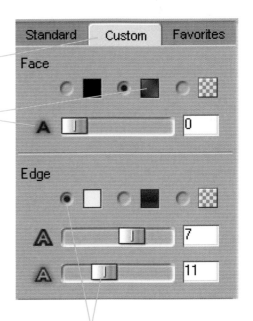

4 Select the colors and effects for the edges of the text

If you are blurring the edges of text, or using a shadow effect, make sure that there is a good contrast between the text color and the edges or shadow color, otherwise the text may become difficult to read.

5 Select the colors and effects for the shadow effect for the text

6 Click here to select the direction for the shadow effect

7 The custom formatting can be previewed here

8 Click OK

9 The custom formatting is applied to the selected text as it is created

Creating favorites

Each time a custom text style is created it is only applied to the currently selected text box. However, it is possible to save custom styles so that they can be used for other text boxes. To do this:

1 Create a custom style and click on the Favorites tab

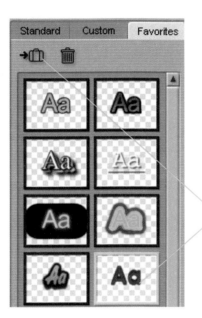

2 Click here to add the current custom style to the Favorites list

3 To apply a style from the Favorites panel, select a text box and double click on the required Favorites style

Advanced formatting

The text manipulation tools can be used to apply more advanced editing techniques to text boxes and, in some cases, to other objects too.

Grouping objects

Two or more text boxes can be grouped together. Once this has been done, editing effects can be applied to both items simultaneously. Graphical objects can also be grouped together with text boxes. To group objects:

1 Select a text box or object

Once objects have been grouped, the objects within the group can be aligned in various ways by using the Align button next to the ungroup one. The same commands can also be applied by selecting Title>Align from the Menu bar.

2 Hold down Ctrl and click on another item so that both are selected

3 Click here to group the objects

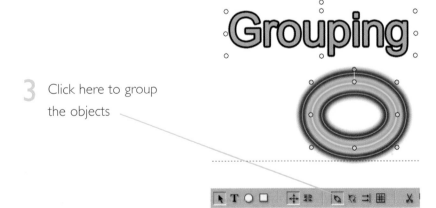

Arranging objects

If objects overlap, the order in which they appear can be altered. To do this:

1 Select an object which is overlapping another

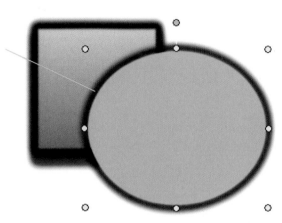

Numerous objects can be arranged together, to create complex, multi-overlapping graphics.

Make sure you select the correct object before the arranging options are applied.

2 Select Title>Layer from the Menu bar and select one of the arrangement options

Bring to Front	Alt +
Send to Back	Alt -
Bring Forward One Layer	Ctrl +
Send Back One Layer	Ctrl -

3 The command is applied to the selected object

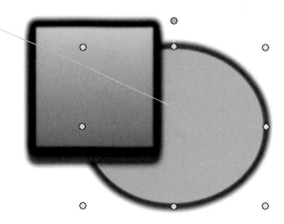

Justifying objects

Objects can be aligned within the Title Editor by using the Justify button:

Objects have to first be selected in order to have justifying applied to them.

Click on one of the nine segments to position the object at that point

Kerning and leading

Kerning and leading are techniques which can be used to change the amount of space between letters and between lines, respectively. To apply kerning and leading:

Kerning can be applied to individual letters rather than just whole words. To do this, highlight the required letters and apply kerning to them. The selected letters appear with their own control points when the kerning tool is selected.

1 Select the Kern and Skew tool

2 Drag here to apply kerning i.e. the space between individual letters

3 Drag here to apply leading i.e. the space between lines

4 The effect is applied to everything in the text box, unless specific text is selected

Title Editor album

The Title Editor album is the area of the Title Editor in which elements can be applied to the title which is being constructed.

The Looks panels

These are to apply styles to text boxes as shown on the previous pages. However, these styles can also be applied to graphical objects such as ellipses and rectangles.

The Background panel

This contains various background styles which can be applied to a title:

Backgrounds can be applied to a title by clicking on them once. To change the background, click once on another one.

Click here to browse to other titles

Pictures panel

This can be used to add still images to a title:

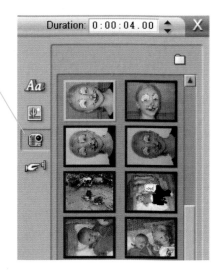

Still images and buttons can be added to a title by double clicking on them or by dragging them from their respective panels onto the Title Editor window.

Buttons panel

This can be used to add buttons when you are creating a menu title:

Buttons are usually added to titles that are created as interactive menus for use with DVDs, S-VCDs or VCDs. For more details about this, see Chapter Eleven.

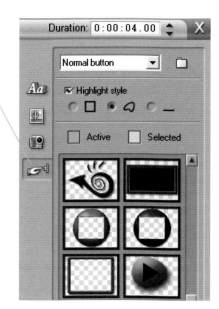

Adding titles and backgrounds

The Title Editor is used to create and edit titles. This chapter looks at the types of titles that can be used within movies and shows how to add and edit them. It also covers the use of backgrounds in conjunction with titles.

Covers

Chapter Eight

Overlay titles

Overlay titles are ones which are placed over existing video clips. To add these:

1. Select a clip on the Storyboard or the Timeline and access the video toolbox

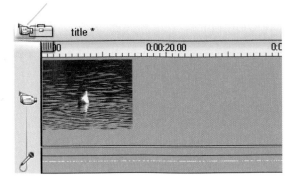

The length of an overlay title can be edited so that it synchronizes with the video clip over which it is placed.

2. Select the titles option

3. Select the Title Overlay button

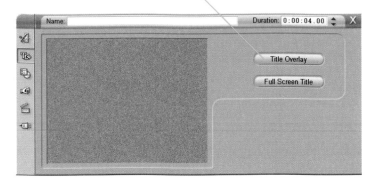

4 In the Title Editor click on a font style and type the required text over the video clip

Make sure there is a good contrast between the font color for the overlay title and the whole of the video clip over which it will appear.

5 Click OK

An overlay title can be dragged onto the main video track, in which case it becomes a full screen title on a black background.

6 The title is placed on the Storyboard or on the title track of the Timeline

7 Preview the title in the Player

Full screen titles

Full screen titles are ones that are created on blank or graphical backgrounds, rather than video clips. To add these:

1 Select a clip on the Storyboard or the Timeline and access the video toolbox

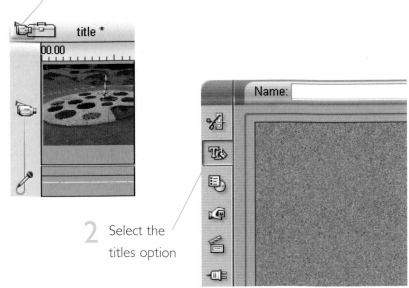

Full screen titles can be used for the credits at the beginning and the end of a movie and also within a movie to convey important pieces of information.

2 Select the titles option

3 Select the Full Screen Title button

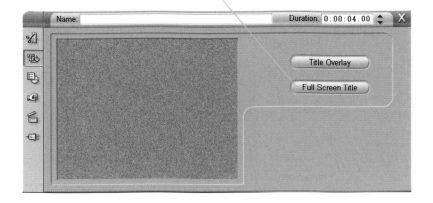

4 In the Title Editor click on a font style and type the required text over the blank background

Full screen titles are placed on the main video track, whereas overlay titles are placed on the titles track. This means that full screen titles play on their own, while overlay titles play simultaneously with video clips.

5 Click OK

Full screen titles can have graphical backgrounds and still images added to them. They do not have to just consist of text on a plain background.

6 The title is placed on the Storyboard or the video track on the Timeline

7 Preview the title in the Player

Preformatted titles

As well as creating your own titles, it is also possible to use those that come bundled with Pinnacle Studio. To do this:

1 Select the titles option and click on a preformatted title

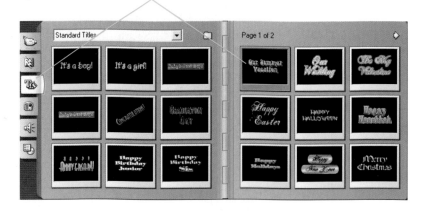

Once a preformatted title has been added to the Timeline, it can still be edited in the same way as any other title.

2 Drag the title onto the Timeline

3 Preview the title in the Player

4 Place the title here on the Timeline to use it as a full screen title

To change a full screen title into an overlay one, drag it from the main video track onto the title track.

5 Place the title here on the Timeline to use it as an overlay title

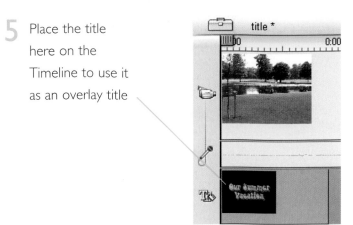

6 The overlay title appears on top of the video clip

Setting title length

The length of time that titles remain on screen is an important issue: you do not want to spend a lot of time crafting beautiful titles, only for them to fly past on the screen so that no-one has time to read them properly. The length of time that titles appear on the screen can be set in either the Title Editor or by editing the title in the Timeline.

Setting length with the Title Editor

Try and ensure that the length of a title is neither too short, so that it whizzes past, or too long, so that people will get bored looking at it. Test titles by viewing them in context with the rest of the movie.

Create a title in the Title Editor or double click on an existing title on the Timeline

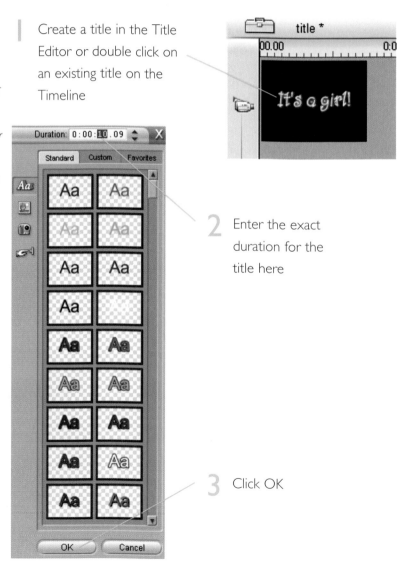

2 Enter the exact duration for the title here

3 Click OK

Setting length with the Timeline

Once a title has been created, its length can be edited in the Timeline, so that it matches exactly any other relevant content in the movie:

1 Select a title on the Timeline by clicking on it once

It is possible to extend the length of an overlay title beyond the end of the final video clip in a movie. This can be useful if you want to keep the title on screen once the movie has finished.

2 Click and drag on the title's border to edit its length

3 Preview the title in the Player to see its full duration

Creating moving titles

In the Title Editor it is possible to create titles that move up the screen from bottom to top (scrolling) or across the screen from right to left (crawling).

Scrolling titles

1 Access the Title Editor and add a background (see pages 128–129 for details)

2 Click here to create a scrolling title

Scrolling titles are the most effective for credits at the beginning or the end of a movie.

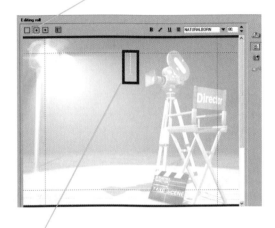

Scrolling titles stop at the point where the top of the text box reaches the top red border line in the Title Editor. In the movie, when the scrolling text reaches this point, the title will end. The text does not scroll all of the way up the screen and disappear at the top.

3 A text box is inserted at the point at which the scrolling title will finish

4 Enter text for the title and click OK

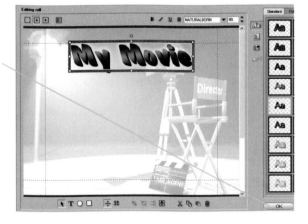

Crawling titles

Crawling titles can be used to give additional information without detracting too much from the video footage. They can be used to create a textual commentary for a movie.

1 Access the Title Editor and add a background

2 Click here to create a crawling title

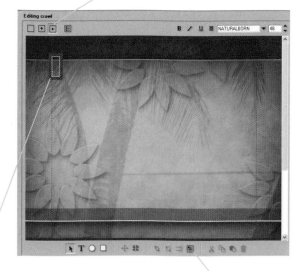

Use the Justify tool to specify the location of the crawling text. The options are top, middle or bottom.

3 A text box is inserted at the point at which the crawling title will finish

4 Click here to select the position of the crawling title

5 Enter text for the title and click OK

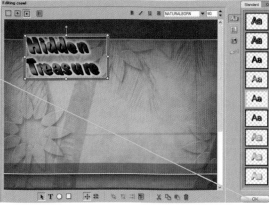

Adding backgrounds

Full screen titles can be placed on graphical backgrounds as well as blank backgrounds. To add backgrounds:

Backgrounds add to the overall file size of a movie, but not to any great extent.

1 Access the video toolbox and open the Title Editor

2 Select the titles option and select the Full Screen Title button

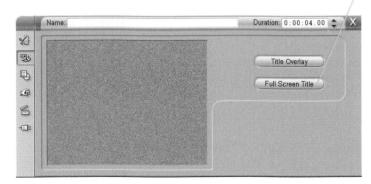

3 Click here to access the backgrounds and click on one once

Backgrounds can also be added by dragging them from the Title Editor album onto the editing window.

4 Add a title

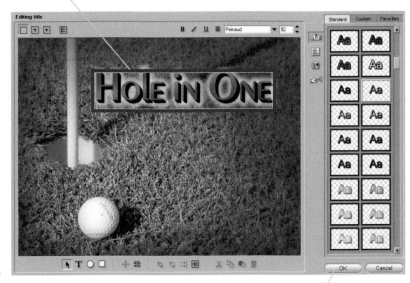

Backgrounds can be added on their own, without a title being included.

5 Click OK

6 Preview the title in the Player

Creating a blank background

On occasions you may want to create a blank background. This could be to insert a pause in a movie or to produce a creative effect with a transition. To create a blank background:

1 Access the Title Editor for the creation of a full screen title

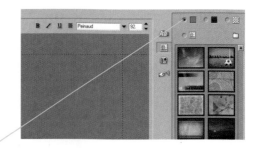

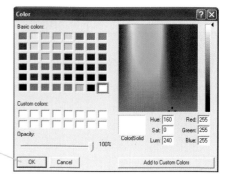

The buttons to the right of the color button can be used to create gradient backgrounds and also backgrounds with varying degrees of transparency.

2 Click here to select a solid color for the background

3 Select a color and click OK

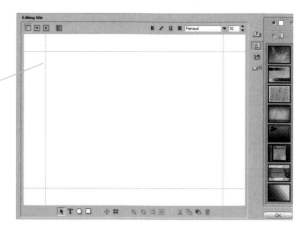

4 The color is applied to the background. Click OK to add this to a movie

Adding still images

Still images can be added to titles, either as backgrounds or to display the images themselves. To do this:

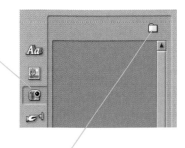

1 Access the Title Editor and click here to access the still images panel in the Title Editor album

Adding still images as titles is a good way of creating a slideshow of digital images. To do this, add each image as a separate title and set the duration accordingly in the duration box. If required, text can be added as a description of each image.

2 Click here to access still images from your hard drive

3 Select an image within a folder and click Open

Resize still images by dragging the corner resizing handles. This will resize the image in proportion. If the middle resizing handles are used, this will make the image appear out of proportion.

4 Double click on an image to add it to a title. The image is inserted at its actual size and can be resized by dragging the resizing handles

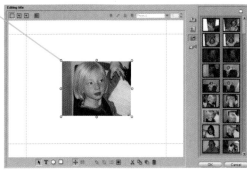

Lower thirds

If you want to add other textual elements, other than titles, then a useful device for assisting with this is lower thirds. A lower third is a graphical element that can be placed at the bottom of the video and then have text placed over the top. This can be particularly useful if you want to add subtitles to video footage.

A lower third is essentially a type of background, that does not take up the whole screen. Lower thirds can be obtained from the Web or from cover discs of digital video magazines.

1 Access the video toolbox and open the Title Editor

2 Add text to the video footage

When working with lower thirds, make sure you create the correct stacking order with the lower third and the text i.e. the lower third should be on the bottom and the text on the layer above it. To do this, select Title>Layer from the Menu bar and select the required stacking option.

3 Click here to access lower third backgrounds on your hard drive

4 Navigate to the folder in which the lower thirds are located, select it, and click Open

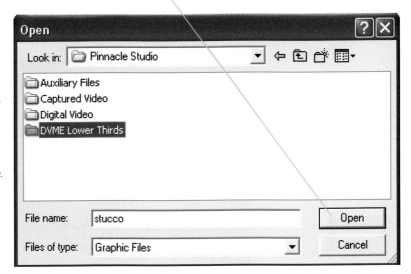

If lower thirds are added from a third party disc, they will be installed in a separate folder on your hard drive.

5 The lower thirds are inserted in the backgrounds panel of the Title Editor

Lower thirds are a good way of emphasizing overlay titles and they can also be used as backgrounds for subtitles.

6 Click once on a lower third to add it to the title. If required, move the lower third so that it is located in the correct position behind the text

By default, a title with a lower third does not automatically match the length of the video clip over which it has been placed. However, once it has been added to the Timeline it can be extended as required.

Lower thirds can be added to full screen and overlay titles.

7 Click OK to add the title with the lower third to the Timeline

8 Preview the lower third in the Player

Adding audio

Pinnacle Studio can be used to add different types of audio to a movie. This chapter looks at the types of audio that can be used and shows how to add them to a movie and edit them. It also shows how to trim the length of audio clips and adjust the volume.

Covers

Chapter Nine

Types of audio

Audio, or sound, can be recorded at the same time as video footage i.e. recording what someone is saying in a video, or it can be added as a separate element at a later stage. There are different types of audio that can be used with digital video:

The synchronous audio track can be used to record a narration for the video footage as it is being captured. However, this could involve talking as you are filming, which can be hazardous. If in doubt, record the narration as a separate track later.

- Synchronous audio. This is the audio that is captured at the same time as the video footage i.e. it is synchronized with the video

- Narration. This is a separate audio track that is recorded independently from the main video track. It can include items such as a spoken commentary

- Sound effects. There are hundreds of different sound effects that can be added to video footage, ranging from wedding bells to car engines, and birds singing to breaking glass

- Background audio. This is usually in the form of background music, that can be added from a source such as a CD

Each audio item occupies a different track on the Timeline:

The items on each track are played simultaneously at the point at which the Scrubber moves over them.

Video

Synchronous audio

Sound effects or narration

Background audio

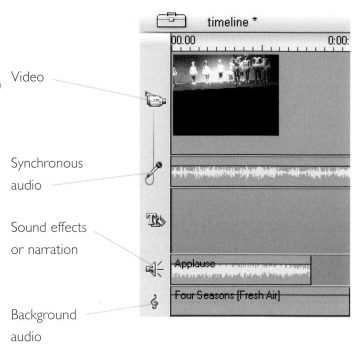

Synchronous audio

Since synchronous audio is captured at the same time as the video footage it is, by default, linked directly to the footage during the editing process. This means that if a video clip is shortened during editing, the synchronous audio will be shortened too.

1 By default, the video and the synchronous audio are the same length

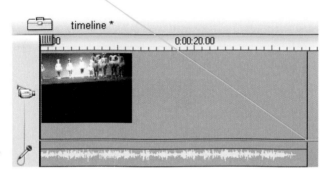

If the synchronous audio is going to be important for the final movie, make sure you are as close as possible to where the audio is being produced. This will ensure that the video camera's microphone picks up the sound as clearly as possible.

2 If the length of the video is edited, the synchronous audio is amended accordingly

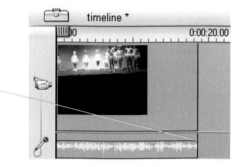

3 However, by clicking here and locking the video track it is possible to edit the synchronous audio track independently from the video one

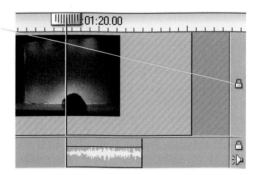

Narration

This is also known as a voice-over and consists of a separately recorded soundtrack that accompanies the video. To create this type of audio track you will need a microphone attached to your computer. If possible, try and use the best microphone you can afford as this will impact on the final quality of the narration. To record narration or a voice-over:

Write out a script for your narration and practise it before you undertake a live recording. Use a stopwatch to time the duration of the narration.

1 Access the audio toolbox and click here to access the narration option

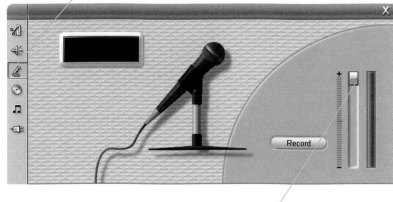

Try not to get too close to the microphone when you are speaking, as this can create a muffled effect in the final recording.

2 Drag this slider to set the recording level

3 Click the Record button

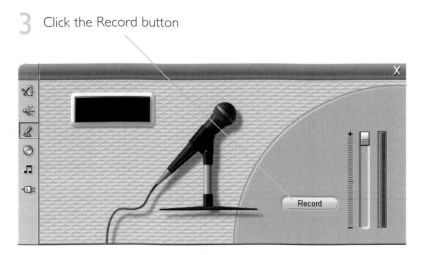

4 A countdown displays how long until recording will start

5 Record the narration and click Stop to finish recording

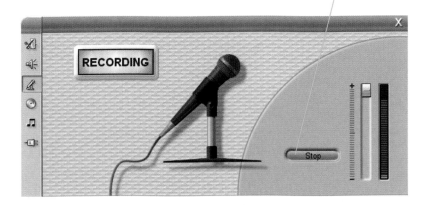

If you are reading a narration from a script, use a document holder to avoid the noise of rustling paper appearing on the soundtrack.

6 The narration is added here on the Timeline

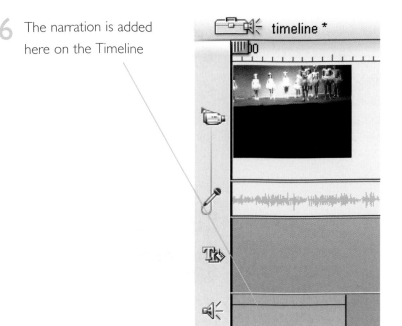

Sound effects

Sound effects can be used to make certain aspects of a video seem more realistic or for adding humorous touches with comic sound effects. Some sound effects are included on the Pinnacle Studio installation disc. To add sound effects:

Additional sound effects can also be downloaded from various websites and obtained from cover discs that come with digital video magazines.

1 Click here to access the sound effects option

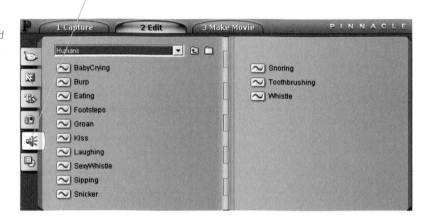

You can record your own sound effects in the same way as recording a narration. However, it may take a little time and practise to perfect this technique.

2 Select an effect and click here in the Player to preview it

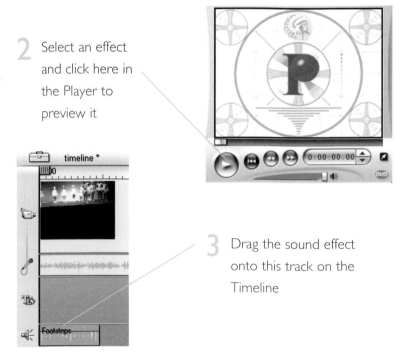

3 Drag the sound effect onto this track on the Timeline

Background music

Background sound, usually in the form of music, can be added to a video to give it an extra dimension. This can either play softly in conjunction with any other audio that is present, or it can be the main, or only, audio that is in the video. Background sound can be added from a sound file stored on your computer or from a CD. To do this:

When adding background audio from a CD, or creating a recorded narration or voice-over, there are certain settings that can be applied before the audio is captured. To access these, select Setup>CD and Voiceover from the Menu bar.

1 Access the audio toolbox

2 Click here to download music from a CD

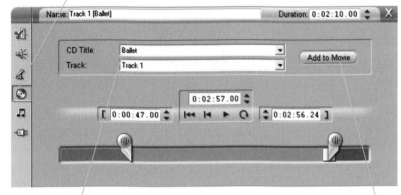

If you are going to be using your video for anything other than personal use, you will need to get permission to use copyrighted music.

3 Enter a name for the CD and select a track

4 Click here to add the clip to the current movie

5 The background sound file is placed here on the Timeline and can be edited accordingly, either on the Timeline or in the audio toolbox

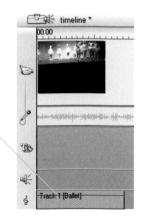

SmartSound

SmartSound is a feature that is unique to Pinnacle Studio. It enables you to create background music that fits the entire duration of a video clip or a whole movie. The music is provided on the Studio CD and it can either be downloaded when the program is installed or it can be accessed directly from the disc. To use SmartSound:

The SmartSound music clips take up a lot of hard disc space. If you are concerned about this, do not download them when you install Studio, but access them from the installation disc when they are required.

1 Select one or more video clips on the Timeline and click here to access the audio toolbox

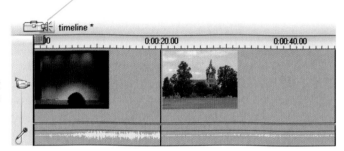

2 Click here to access the SmartSound panel

3 Select a Style, Song and Version

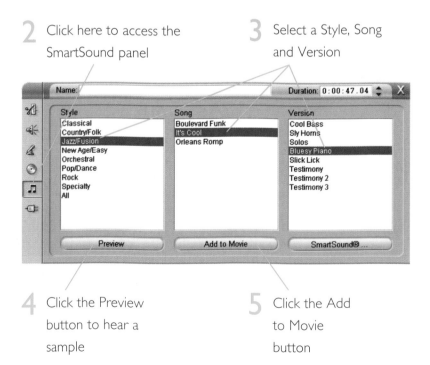

4 Click the Preview button to hear a sample

5 Click the Add to Movie button

6 The name for the music is added here. Highlight this and overtype to change it

7 The duration of the music is automatically adjusted to match the length of the selected clip(s)

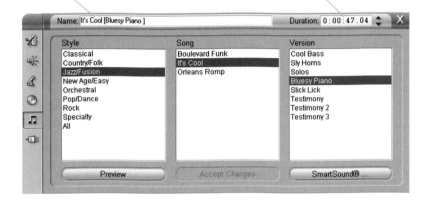

8 The SmartSound music is added to the background music track and it matches the length of the selected movie clip(s)

If you only want the SmartSound music in the movie, the video soundtrack can be muted. See pages 149–150 for details.

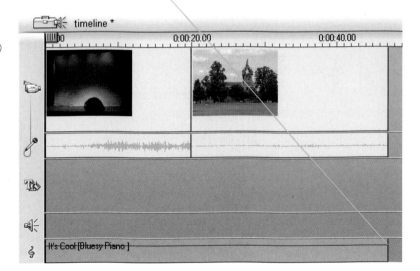

Audio effects

Effects can be added to audio elements in a video and it is a similar process to adding them to video clips. The effects include noise reduction (which can reduce unwanted background noise and also the faint hiss that can accompany video recordings) to effects such as reverb. To add audio effects:

The Noise Reduction category contains preset options for reducing noise from video recorded outdoors and indoors.

1 Open an audio clip in the audio toolbox and click here

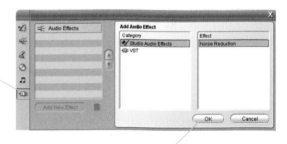

2 Select a category and an effect and click OK

3 Select the attributes for the effect and click here to add it to the clip

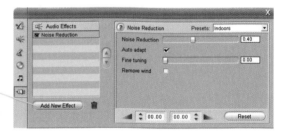

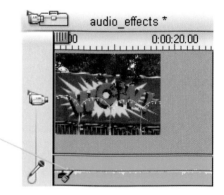

The audio effects under the VST category are third party plug-ins that can be used within Studio. Some of them are demo versions and information about the full versions can be found on the Pinnacle website at www.pinnaclesys.com

4 The audio clip can be previewed in the Player. On the Timeline the presence of audio effects are denoted by the relevant icons under the clip

Adjusting audio levels

All of the audio tracks that are included in a video can have their levels altered, i.e. made louder or quieter. This can be done through the audio toolbox and also by editing the audio track in the Timeline. To adjust audio levels using the audio toolbox:

1 Access the audio toolbox

2 Click here to access the audio levels controls

To increase or decrease the volume of one part of video without affecting the rest of it, split the video clip so that the required item is a single clip. Then select it and change the volume with the audio levels controls.

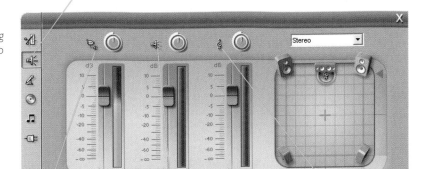

Synchronous audio

Narration and sound effects audio

Background audio

Any changes to audio levels that are made in the audio toolbox are simultaneously applied on the Timeline.

Drag here to change the volume for an entire track

Drag here to change the volume for an individual clip

Adjusting audio levels with the Timeline

Audio levels can also be adjusted on the Timeline. This is effective for creating a fade in or fade out effect. To do this:

1   Click and drag at the ends of the volume line to decrease or increase the volume of the entire audio track

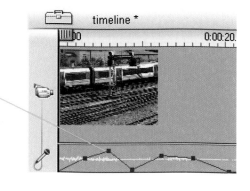

Adjustment handles can only be added by clicking and dragging on the volume line in the Timeline. If you just click on it, this will have no effect.

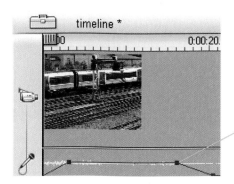

2   Click and drag on the volume line, then move it back to its original position. This creates an adjustment handle. This stays in place if another part of the line is moved

3   Each time the volume line is altered, an adjustment handle is added. These can be used to increase or decrease the volume at different points

Balance control

In addition to being able to alter the volume of audio clips, it is also possible to adjust their balance i.e. the point at which they are played through a speaker system once the final movie has been published. It is possible to set the balance for both stereo systems and also surround sound systems that are used in home cinema set-ups. To set the audio balance:

Each audio track can be moved independently from the others. To do this, click on one of the audio track icons until it becomes illuminated and then drag it into position.

1 Click here to select whether the balance will be for stereo or surround sound

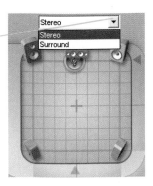

2 For a stereo system, drag the audio tracks horizontally between the two speakers

If an audio track has been muted, or is not present, then the relevant icon will be visible but it will be grayed out.

3 For a surround sound system, drag the audio tracks within the triangle in the middle of the speakers

4 The position of each track can also be altered by dragging here

Fading audio

Audio clips can also be faded in or out using the audio toolbox. To do this:

1 Select an audio clip and access the audio toolbox

2 Click here to select the volume options

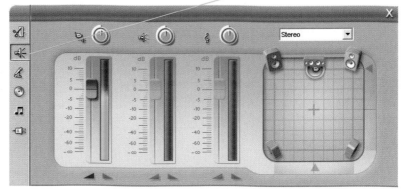

Fade in or out effects in the audio toolbox are applied at the point at which the Scrubber is located on the Timeline.

3 Move the Scrubber to the start of the clip and click here. This will create a fade in effect

4 Move the Scrubber to the end of the clip and click here. This will create a fade out effect

Muting audio

When working with audio there will probably be times when you want to mute the sound at certain points within the video. The audio within individual clips can be muted, as can an entire audio track.

Muting a clip

1 Access the volume controls in the audio toolbox

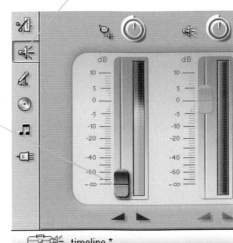

2 Drag the volume slider to the bottom. Make sure you select the slider for the relevant audio item

Muted audio can be reinstated by dragging the relevant slider in the audio toolbox or by dragging the volume line on the Timeline.

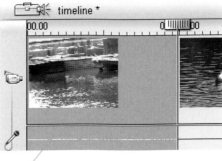

3 The volume level for the selected clip is moved to the bottom of the clip in the Timeline. This indicates that the audio has been muted. The volume of other clips on the same track are unaffected

Muting an entire audio track

1 Look at the Timeline and select the audio track you want to mute. Access the volume option in the audio toolbox

2 Click here to mute the selected audio track throughout the current movie

If you decide you want to use the audio from a particular clip on a track that has been muted, click the mute audio button so that the red line disappears and then mute the audio for individual clips within the track, rather than the entire track.

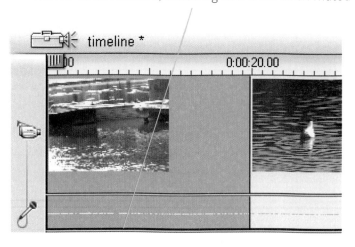

3 The volume line for all of the audio on the selected track is moved to the bottom, indicating that it has been muted

timeline *

0:00:20.00

Trimming audio

The length of audio clips can be trimmed in the same way as trimming video footage. This can be done in the clip properties section of the audio toolbox or on the Timeline.

Trimming in the audio toolbox

The synchronous audio track cannot be trimmed without first locking the video track. See next page for details.

1 Select an audio clip and click here in the audio toolbox

2 Drag the Scrubber to the point at which you want the audio clip to begin

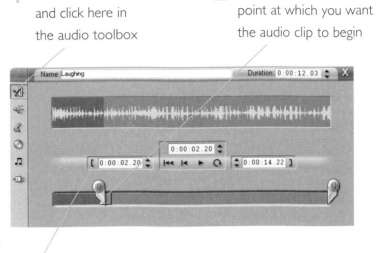

Audio tracks can be trimmed in the video toolbox as well as the audio toolbox.

3 Click here to set the Mark In point of the audio track

4 Drag the Scrubber to the point at which you want the audio clip to end

5 Click here to set the Mark Out point of the audio track

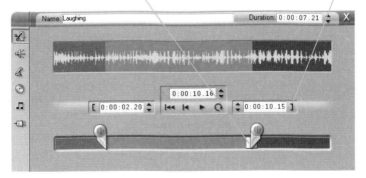

Trimming on the Timeline

Select an audio clip and
position the cursor over
either border until a
single- or double-headed
arrow appears

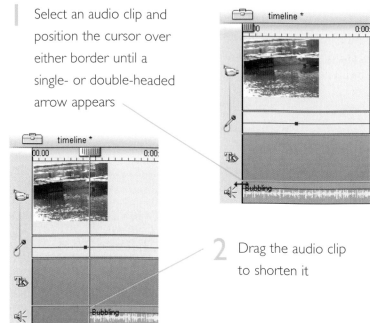

2 Drag the audio clip
to shorten it

Trimming audio independently

To trim synchronous audio independently from the video track:

Click here to lock
the video track

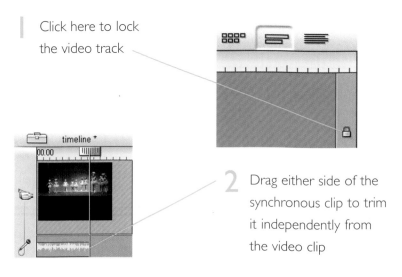

2 Drag either side of the
synchronous clip to trim
it independently from
the video clip

Still images

This chapter looks at how still images can be used within a movie. It shows how to obtain digital photographs and how to grab individual frames from video footage. It also covers adding images to a movie and editing them once they are included.

Covers

Chapter Ten

Obtaining digital photos

Still images can be added to movies from either a digital camera, a scanner or as a frame that has been grabbed from video footage. Digital images can be obtained from either the hard drive or directly from a digital device. To obtain digital still images:

1 | Click here in the Album

2 | Click here to access images from the hard drive

3 | Select an image in a folder

To open a folder of images in Pinnacle Studio, the folder has to be opened and an individual image selected.

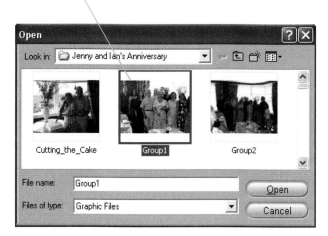

or

Click here to access a
digital device, if one is
connected

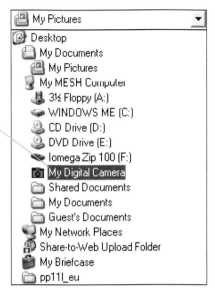

 *If you are
capturing digital
images for use in
a movie, make
sure you do so at
the highest available resolution.
This will improve the quality
when it is viewed in the
completed movie.*

4 Click Open to add
the selected images
to the Album

5 The images appear
in the Album

Grabbing frames

Individual frames can be grabbed either directly from a video camera or from video footage that has already been downloaded.

Grabbing from downloaded footage

| Select a video clip and open the video toolbox. Click here to access the frame grab options

By default, video frame grabs are 4 seconds in duration.

2 Click here to grab a frame from the currently selected video clip

Click on the Reduce Flicker box to ensure that the frame grab is as clear as possible.

3 The grabbed frame is the one displayed in the Player

4 Click here to add the frame grab to the current movie

 For greater precision in grabbing frames, stop the preview in the Player at the point where you want to grab a frame. Then click the Grab button. The frame that is visible in the Player will be the one that is grabbed.

5 The frame grab is placed in front of the video clip from which it was obtained

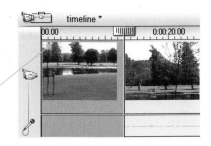

6 Click here to save the frame grab to your hard drive

7 Navigate to the folder in which you want to save the grabbed image and click Save

Grabbing from a video camera

1 Connect and turn on the video camera and click here in the video toolbox

Frames grabbed directly from digital video footage are usually a higher quality than those grabbed from an analog camera that is then converted to digital.

2 Click here to access the connected video camera

Most digital video cameras have the facility to capture still images onto a memory card within the camera. This is a useful alternative to grabbing frames after the video has been captured.

3 Click here to play the video from the camera

4 Click here to pause the video from the camera

5 Click here to grab a video frame as it is playing

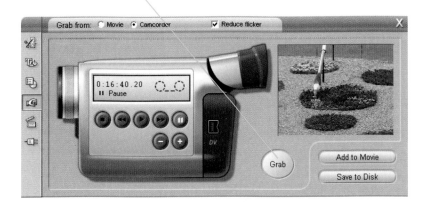

6 The grabbed frame is the one currently displayed in the Player

Save frame grabs in the same folder (or sub-folder) as your video files. This keeps all of the video related items in the same place.

7 Click here to add the frame grab to the current movie

8 Click here to save the frame grab to your hard drive

Editing still images

Once still images have been added to a movie they are treated in the same way as titles and can be edited accordingly. To do this:

1 Double click on a still image on the Timeline or the Storyboard to open it in the Title Editor

2 The image can be edited in the Title Editor in the same way as creating or editing a new title. Click OK to apply the changes

Regardless of their original size, frame grabs that are used for title backgrounds will cover the full area of the title.

3 The editing changes are visible on the still image on the Timeline or the Storyboard

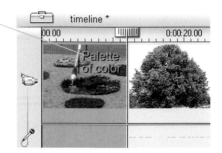

Creating menus

Graphical menus are now a common feature of commercial DVDs. They allow you to move immediately to specific points in a movie. This chapter shows how you can add interactive menus to video footage that is going to be output to a CD or a DVD. It explains the concept of menus and shows how they can be created and edited.

Covers

Chapter Eleven

Menus overview

If you are going to be publishing your completed video to CD or DVD then you may want to include a menu at the beginning of it. This is a useful device to enable the user to move between sections of the video, without having to watch it all or using fast forward to get to the desired part. Menus can be used for the following:

- To move to the beginning of the video

- To move to sections (chapters) within the video

- Move to other menus within the video

Menus can either be created manually or they can be added using preset designs. Menus usually consist of a background image (which can be static or animated) and buttons which are added to give a menu its functionality.

Menus work most effectively when they are included with a movie that has been created on a DVD. This way the DVD handset can be used to control the menu's functionality.

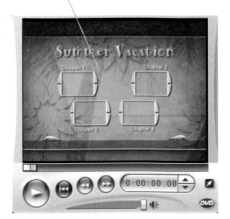

Menus appear here on the timeline and they are denoted by the M tag

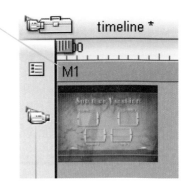

Creating a menu

Once all of the content has been added to a movie, an interactive menu can be added at the start. To do this:

Content can also be added to a movie once a menu has been created. If this happens, the menu will need to be updated to include the new content.

1 Create a movie of one or more video clips. Click here in the Album

In the menus panel of the Album, animated menus are denoted by a yellow icon at the bottom right corner of the menu.

2 Select an appropriate design and drag it onto the Timeline

3 A dialog box appears, asking if you want links to each scene of the movie. If you do, click Yes

If you have a very long movie, with a lot of scenes, it is probably best not to have links to every scene. This would just create a very large menu.

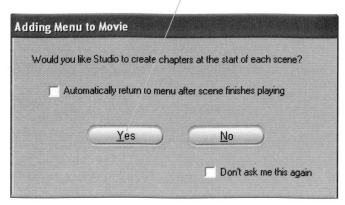

4 The menu appears at the beginning of the movie, with buttons that correspond to each scene (chapter) in the movie

In menu notation, "M" stands for "Menu" and "C" stands for "Chapter".

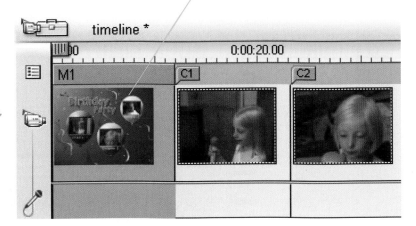

5 The menu can be previewed in the Player. Click here to access the DVD preview function

For details of the DVD preview function see Chapter Three, page 43.

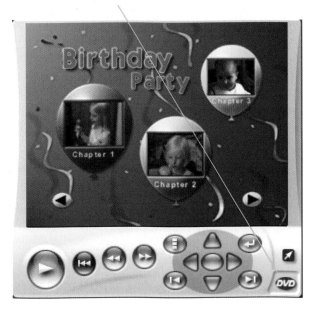

Editing menu functionality

Once a menu has been created it can still be edited. This includes editing the way it functions and also its content. To edit the functionality:

1 Double click on the menu buttons on the Timeline to open this part of the menu in the video toolbox

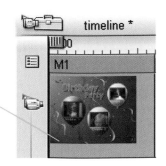

2 Click here to add chapter markers automatically

3 Click here to add chapter markers manually

Display markers are small squares displayed in the video toolbox that indicate the destination of a button once it is clicked. For instance, if the display marker for a button is C2 then the movie will jump to Chapter 2 when this button is clicked.

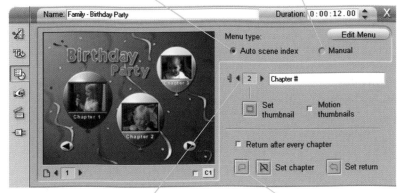

5 Click here to move between the pages of the menu (if more than one)

4 Click here to display markers for where each button is targeted

6 Click here to enable animated video for the buttons in the menu

Animated buttons only appear in the final published video, not in the preview window. This is because the video has to be rendered before all of its functions can be displayed.

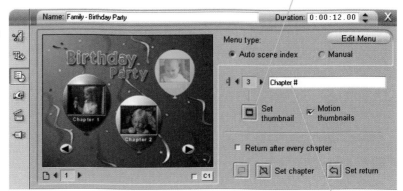

7 Click here to select a button and enter text to give it a new name

8 Click here to select a chapter link for the selected button. This will create a link on the Timeline for the currently selected video clip

9 Click here to delete a chapter link for the selected button. This will delete a link on the Timeline for the currently selected video clip

A Return to Menu button causes the movie to return to the main menu when it reaches the end of the video clip in which it is inserted.

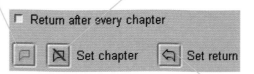

10 Click here to insert a Return to Menu button at the end of the currently selected video clip

Menu content

In addition to editing the functionality of a menu, it is also possible to edit all aspects of the content. To do this:

1   Double click on the menu to open it in the video toolbox. Click here to edit the content of the menu

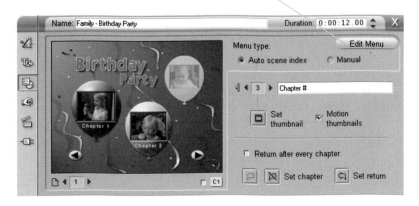

Menus are essentially titles with additional functionality.

2   Click on a text box and highlight the text by dragging over it. Overtype to change the text

3 Click here to select a new background for the menu

Click on the folder icon in the Background window to browse to an image on your hard drive to use as a background.

4 Click once on a background to replace the existing one

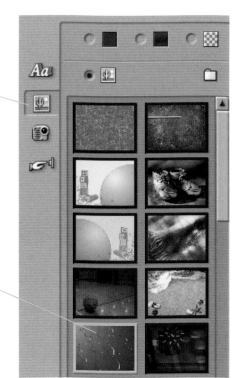

5 Click here to select an image to add to the menu

6 Double click on an image to add it to the menu

Creating buttons

Once the graphical content has been created or added for a menu, the interactive buttons can then be included. Buttons can be used to perform different tasks. To add buttons:

1 Open the menu in the video toolbox and access the menu editing window as shown on page 167

Buttons can be created from the preset designs or existing graphical objects or images can be turned into buttons. To do this, select them in the editing menu window and select a button type from the options in Step 4 on this page.

2 Select an existing button and click once on a new button style to apply it to the menu

3 With nothing selected, double click on a button to add it to the menu

The options for buttons are: Not a button, which means no functionality is applied; Normal button, which can be linked to chapters in a movie; Thumbnail button, which creates an image for the button with the currently selected frame on the Timeline; and Previous and Next buttons, which can be used to access other pages within the main menu (if applicable).

5 Click OK

4 Click here to select a state for the button

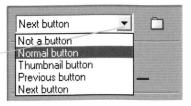

Creating menus manually

If you do not want to use preset menu designs, you can create them from scratch. This can be done at the beginning of a video project, or once you have inserted clips into your project. To create a menu:

1 Open the video toolbox

3 Click Create Menu

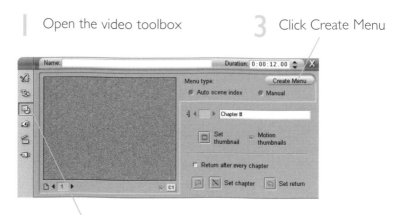

2 Click here to create a new menu

4 Select the Open the Menu Editor option and click OK

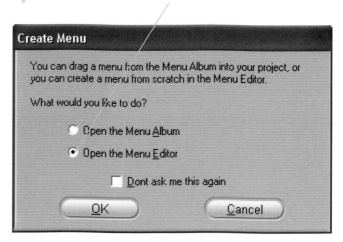

Create Menu

You can drag a menu from the Menu Album into your project, or you can create a menu from scratch in the Menu Editor.

What would you like to do?

○ Open the Menu Album

● Open the Menu Editor

☐ Dont ask me this again

OK   Cancel

5 Add content for the menu in the same way as editing content for a preset menu

Editing chapter markers

The video toolbox and the Timeline can be used to create and edit chapter markers.

Adding chapter markers

| Access the menu in the video toolbox

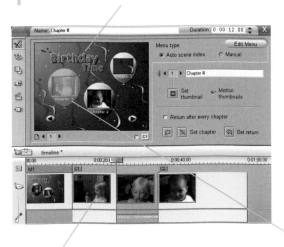

3 Right click on a video clip on the Timeline. Select Set Disc Chapter to create a link between the selected button and the video clip

2 Click on a button in the menu

If a chapter marker is dragged onto a new clip, this does not automatically update the marker that is currently there. This has to be done by dragging the marker over a different clip.

Arranging chapter markers

| Click on a chapter marker on the Timeline so that it turns blue

2 Drag the marker to a different location

Deleting chapter markers

1 Click on a chapter marker on the Timeline so that it turns blue

When deleting chapter markers, make sure you select the marker, rather than the video clip to which it is attached.

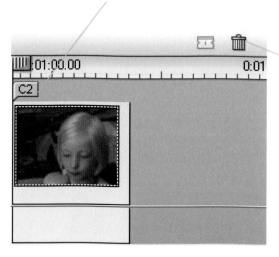

2 Click on the wastebasket to delete the chapter marker. (Or right click on the marker and select Delete from the menu)

Setting Return to Menu markers

If you have a long video, or several different videos on the same disc, it is useful to be able to return to the main menu from various points on the disc. To do this:

Once the Return to Menu function has accessed the main menu the movie will remain at this point until another button is activated.

1 Right click on a video clip and select Set Return to Menu

Go to Title/Menu Editor

Clip Properties

Set Disc Chapter

Set Return to Menu

2 The Return to Menu marker is inserted at the end of the clip. When the Scrubber reaches this point the main menu will be accessed

Adding multiple menus

It is possible to create a file containing several different movies and link them together through the use of menus. This is done by creating one main menu which has links to the chapters of the first movie and also links to other menus for subsequent movies. To do this:

Multiple menus is a good option for creating a disc with one main movie feature and several smaller, related, items. The main menu can be used to jump to other menus that are connected to the smaller features. This is how professional DVDs are produced, with a menu to the main feature and also to the menus for the movies containing all of the additional material.

1 Compile a movie and add a menu with buttons linked to chapter markers

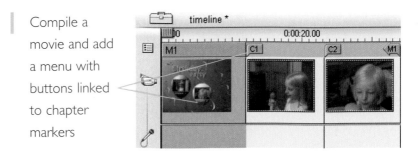

2 Add new video clips for the second movie

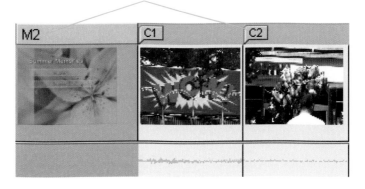

3 Add a menu at the beginning of the second movie. Insert buttons and chapter markers as required

4 Double click on the first menu on the Timeline and click the Edit Menu button in the video toolbox

The main menu i.e. M1, is the one that contains links to chapters in the main movie and also links to menus for smaller movies, all contained within the same file.

5 Add a new button and return to the video toolbox

6 Select the new button and right click on the second menu on the Timeline and select Set Disc Chapter. The menu structure is displayed. In this example the M2 button is linked to the menu at the beginning of the second set of video clips

Publishing

This chapter looks at the various ways in which completed movies can be published in Pinnacle Studio. These include publishing for the Web and publishing onto disc. Each option is covered, including the specific settings for each one.

Covers

Chapter Twelve

Publishing overview

When video footage has been edited and saved in Pinnacle Studio, it is done so in the proprietary Studio file format. As such, the file in this state is of little use as far as displaying it is concerned. It cannot be viewed on another computer, unless it too has Studio installed. At this point, the video footage has to be converted into another format, depending on how the video is going to be used. In the digital video editing process this is known as publishing. The methods for publishing digital video include:

- Digital video tape. This can be used to publish the edited footage back onto the digital video tape from where it came. This requires the digital video camera to be connected to a computer

- AVI (Audio Video Interleaved). A format popular for use on a Windows system

- MPEG. One of the most popular video formats. It can be used when creating VCDs, S-VCDs and DVD. There are two main types, MPEG-1 and MPEG-2

- Streaming. This creates a file that can be used for viewing the video over the Web. It uses extensive compression to make the file as small as possible and also uses the MPEG file format

VCDs, S-VCDs and DVDs use the MPEG file format. VCDs use MPEG-1, while S-VCDs and DVDs use MPEG-2.

- VCD. This is a format for copying onto a CD. It can then be viewed on a computer's CD or DVD drive or on a home DVD player connected to a television. However, the quality is inferior to that of a DVD

- S-VCD. This is another format for copying onto a CD. It allows for greater flexibility when creating the menu for the CD. It can be played on a computer's CD or DVD drive and some home DVD players

- DVD. This is the highest quality for creating discs for viewing on a DVD player. It produces larger file sizes than either VCD or S-VCD and a DVD recorder is required to create the DVDs

Publishing options

The publishing options for Pinnacle Studio are contained within the Make Movie section of the program. This can be used to select the format in which a movie is published and also to specify settings for each format. To use the Make Movie options:

When publishing a movie a new file is created. This will be saved into the same location on your hard drive as the original Studio file from which the new format is created. If the Studio file has not yet been saved, you will be prompted to do this before the new format is created.

1 Click here to select a publishing format

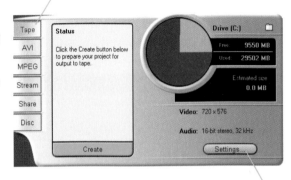

2 Click here to select settings for each format

Once a publishing format has been selected and activated there is usually a considerable delay before the software starts creating the video file or disc. This is because the video first has to be rendered. Rendering is the process of identifying and processing all of the components of the video so that they play correctly in the final published version. Depending on the size of a movie, and the format in which it is being published, rendering can take several hours.

3 Select the required settings and click OK

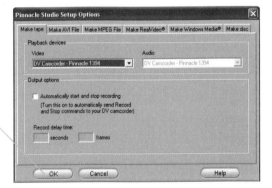

4 Click the Create button to publish a movie in the selected format

Output to tape

Outputting to tape involves copying your edited video footage back onto the original tape. To do this:

The Tape section also has an option for selecting any video file from your hard drive and using this as the source file for copying back to tape.

1 Select the Tape button in the Make Movie window

2 Select the options for how the video is going to be copied onto tape. Click OK

If you are copying video back onto a tape, make sure that you do not copy over existing footage that you want to keep.

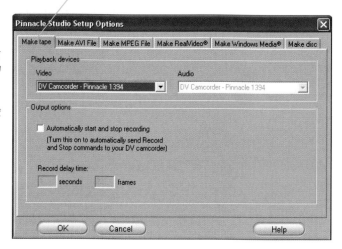

Tape settings
The settings for publishing to tape include:

It can take a bit of trial and error to get the precise timing in the Record Delay Time boxes, as it can vary between different video cameras.

- Type of device to which the video and audio is going to be recorded back to i.e. the type of video camera

- Automatically start and stop recording. Check this box on to start the recording process as soon as the movie has finished rendering. There may be a small delay between when the record command is sent and when recording actually starts. This can be compensated for by entering a value in the Record Delay Time boxes

Output to AVI

AVI (Audio Video Interleaved) is a common video format. Although it produces large file sizes, it can be played on a wide range of computers. When creating AVI files there are a number of options for compressing the video footage. These can decrease the file size, but this is at the expense of the quality. To create AVI files:

1. Select the AVI button in the Make Movie window

2. Select the options for creating the AVI file. These include compression, size and audio settings. Click OK

The AVI format is a useful option if the published movie is intended for distribution to a range of different Windows-based PCs.

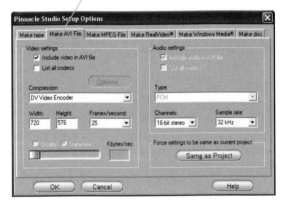

Experiment with the different AVI compression settings to get the best combination of file size and image quality for the use to which a movie is going to be put.

AVI settings

The settings for publishing AVI files include:

- Compression. This is a list of compression settings (codecs) for the published AVI file. Different ones can be used according to how the published file is going to be viewed

- Width and height. This determines the physical size of the published file

- Frame rate. This can be set for the TV standard on which the file is going to be viewed

- Audio settings

Output to MPEG

The MPEG (Motion Pictures Experts Group) format is another file format for displaying video on computers and also for burning onto CDs or DVDs. Two of the versions of MPEG are: MPEG-1 and MPEG-2. MPEG-2 produces the higher quality and this is used for items such as DVDs and S-VCDs. MPEG-1 is used for items such as streaming over the Internet and VCDs. To create MPEG files:

1   Select the MPEG button in the Make Movie window

MPEG-1 files can be published up to 384 x 288 pixels in size and MPEG-2 can be published up to 720 x 576 pixels in size.

2   Select the options for creating the MPEG file. Click OK

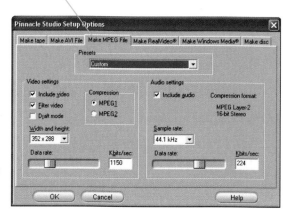

Both MPEG-1 and MPEG-2 files can be played in the Windows Media Player, version 8 or later.

MPEG settings
The settings for publishing MPEG files include:

- Compression. MPEG video files can be compressed using MPEG-1 or MPEG-2 compression. The latter creates higher quality, and larger, files

- Width and height. This is the size at which the movie can be viewed. It is measured in pixels.

- Data rate. This can be set for video and audio. The higher the data rate the higher the quality

- Audio settings. These include the sample rate and the data rate

Output for streaming

Streaming is a technique for playing video files over the Web. To do this successfully, video files have to be compressed as much as possible. This results in much smaller file sizes than for formats such as AVI, but the quality is not as good. The two main options for streaming over the Web are to create a file for the Windows Media Player or the RealVideo Player.

Streaming for Windows Media Player

The Windows Media Player is free and is bundled with programs such as Windows XP. It can also be downloaded from the Microsoft website at www.microsoft.com

1. Select the Stream button in the Make Movie window and select the Windows Media button

2. Select the options for Windows Media Player files. Click OK

Both of the streaming options can be used to email video to specific recipients. To do this, click on the envelope icon in the Stream section of the Make Movie window.

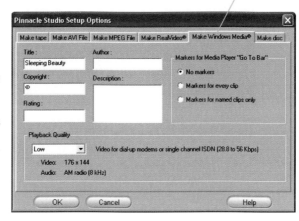

Windows Media Player settings

- File information. This includes details relating to the movie, but they are not visible to most users

- Playback quality. This is determined by how the movie is going to be accessed on the Web. For a slow connection, a low video quality is required, or on a fast connection a higher quality can be used

- Media Player markers. Markers can be inserted so that users can jump to the beginning of a video clip when viewing them in a Web browser

Streaming for RealVideo Player

1 Select the Stream button in the Make Movie window and select the RealVideo button

2 Select the options for RealVideo files. Click OK

The RealVideo Player is free and can be downloaded from the RealNetworks website at www.real.com

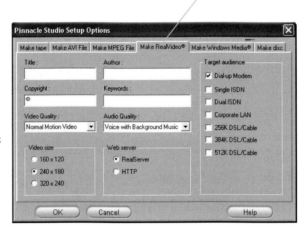

The RealVideo format is a popular one for displaying video within websites.

RealVideo Player settings

- File information. Similar to Windows Media Player

- Video quality. This can be used to create a balance between image quality and the frame rate of the video when it is being viewed

- Audio quality. This is the method for saving the audio

- Video size. This is the size at which the video will be displayed

- Web server. This is the type of Web server on which your video is going to be stored. If in doubt, contact your Web hosting service provider

- Target audience. This is the method by which users will be accessing your video. The quicker the connection the higher the quality of video that can be used

Output for sharing

Pinnacle Studio contains a publishing option for sharing video clips on the Web. The clips are compressed and then uploaded to the Pinnacle website where they can be viewed by anyone who has the password for the specific page within the site. To share video clips:

1 Select the Share button in the Make Movie window

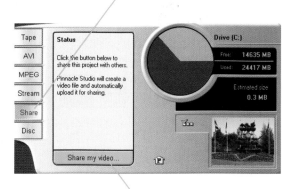

By default, the first frame of a movie is the one that is displayed once a movie has been uploaded for sharing. To change this, move to the frame in the movie you want to be displayed and click on the Set Thumbnail button:

2 Click here to upload the current movie to the Pinnacle website

3 If you have already registered, enter your registration details here

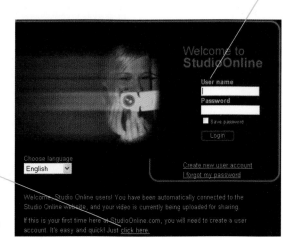

If you forget your login details, Pinnacle will email them to you. To do this, click on the "I forgot my password" link.

4 If you have not registered, click here and follow the onscreen instructions

5 Select a style for displaying the video

Only the people to whom you send the link will be able to view your movie. It will not be universally available for everyone to see.

6 Enter details of the person with whom you want to share the video

You can select a date for when you want the notification email to be sent and you can also ask to be notified when the recipient has accessed the email.

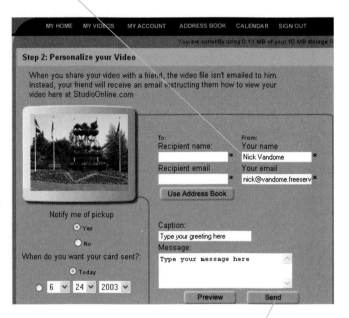

7 Click Send

...cont'd

8 The recipient is sent an email, containing a link to the Pinnacle website. Once it has been activated, the recipient can view the video

When viewing a video on the Pinnacle website, there are options for doing so with either the Windows Media Player or the RealVideo Player.

9 The Share status box displays details of when the video has been uploaded to the Pinnacle website

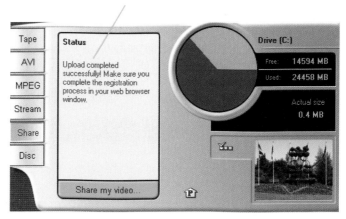

Output to disc

There are three options for publishing movies onto disc within Pinnacle Studio. These are VCD, S-VCD and DVD. The first two of these are recorded onto CDs while the third is recorded onto DVDs. To publish a movie to disc:

1 Select the Disc button in the Make Movie window

2 Click on a disc type and select the required options. Click OK

Not all types of CDs play on all DVD players. Check the DVD's specifications to see if there are any types of disc that it does not play.

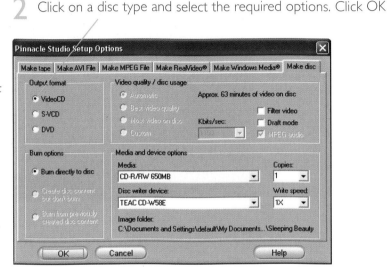

VCDs can hold approximately 1 hour of video footage on a CD.

S-VCDs can hold approximately 30 minutes of video footage on a CD.

DVDs can hold up to 2 hours of video footage depending on the quality settings.

Disc settings

The settings for publishing to disc include:

- Output format. This can be used to select either the VCD, the S-VCD or the DVD option

- Burn options. These can be used to determine the process for burning the disc. Each format displays different options

- Video quality. This can be used to determine the quality of the published video. This in turn can affect the amount of video that can be stored on the disc

- Media and device options. These determine the device to be used to create the disc. Different options are available for the different disc formats

Index

E

F

H

Hollywood FX. *See* Transitions: Hollywood FX

I

i-Link. *See* FireWire
IEEE 1394. *See* FireWire
Input formats
   Digital8   12
   MicroMV   12
   MiniDV   12
Insert editing. *See* Clips: Editing: Insert editing

J

J-cut split editing. *See* Clips: Editing: J-cut split editing

L

L-cut split editing. *See* Clips: Editing: L-cut split editing
Laptops   12
Lower thirds. *See* Titles: Adding lower thirds

M

Make Movie mode   16
Menu
   Editing   167
Menu bar   41
   Album menu   41
   Edit menu   41
   File menu   41
   Help menu   41
   Setup menu   41
   Toolbox menu   41
   View menu   41
Menus   40. *See also* Video toolbox: Options: Menus; Video
    toolbox: Tools: Menus
   Buttons
    Creating   169
   Chapter markers   171
    Adding   171
    Arranging   171
    Deleting   172
   Chapters   164
   Creating   163
    Manually   170
   Editing   165
   Functionality   165
   Multiple
    Adding   173
   Overview   162
MicroMV. *See* Input formats: MicroMV
Microsoft
   Windows XP   27
MiniDV. *See* Input formats: MiniDV
Motion Pictures Experts Group. *See* MPEG
Movie Window   15
Movies
   Creating   62
MPEG   9, 13, 176, 180

Working with clips

This chapter looks at how various types of clips can be used to create new movies in Pinnacle Studio. This includes all of the types of clips that are available in Studio, but particularly video clips. Adding and editing clips is covered, as well as more advanced features such as insert editing and split editing.

Covers

Chapter Five

Creating a movie

Once a video file has been downloaded into Pinnacle Studio it is just the raw footage from the video camera in its unedited state. At this point it cannot be edited or published from within Studio. To do this, the individual video clips have to be collated into a new movie within Studio. The video clips are the building blocks of the final movie construction. They have to be added to the Timeline or the Storyboard in order for them to become part of a new Studio movie.

The raw video footage is displayed here. At this point there is no content to make up a new Studio movie

To create a new movie file in Pinnacle select File>New Project from the Menu bar.

The original video file has to be present in order for a clip from it to be visible on the Timeline or the Storyboard. If the original file is deleted from the hard drive, the clip will not be visible in the movie, even if the movie has already been saved.

Once a clip is added to the Timeline or the Storyboard, the new Studio movie contains content

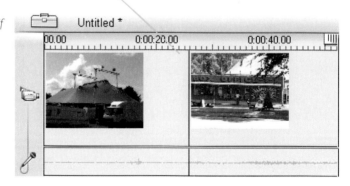